IMAGES OF POSSIBILITY

Alison Wertheimer

IMAGES OF POSSIBILITY

Creating learning opportunities
for adults with mental health difficulties

Alison Wertheimer

Published by the
National Institute of Adult Continuing Education (England and Wales)
21 De Montfort Street
Leicester LE1 7GE
Company registration number 2603322
Charity registration number 1002775

The NIACE website on the Internet is http://www.niace.org.uk

Details of publications by FEDA are available from:
FEDA, Coombe Lodge, Blagdon, Bristol BS18 6RG

First published in 1997
© NIACE, 1997

Cataloguing in Publications Data
A CIP record for this title is available from the British Library

ISBN 1 86201 032 3

Designed and typeset by Boldface
Cover illustration by Steven Cull
Printed and bound in Great Britain by Redwood Books

CONTENTS

ACKNOWLEDGEMENTS   vii

THE FEDA/NIACE PROJECT   ix

VOICES   xi

CHAPTER ONE
SETTING THE SCENE   1

CHAPTER TWO
WHICH LABEL?   21

CHAPTER THREE
PARTICIPATION AND EMPOWERMENT   32

CHAPTER FOUR
OVERCOMING BARRIERS TO SUCCESSFUL LEARNING   46

CHAPTER FIVE
MAKING IT HAPPEN   58

CHAPTER SIX
BUILDING ALLIANCES   72

CHAPTER SEVEN
FUNDING   84

CHAPTER EIGHT
GETTING IN: ACCESS, GUIDANCE AND ASSESSMENT   98

CHAPTER NINE
STAYING THE COURSE: SUPPORT FOR LEARNING   117

CHAPTER TEN
GETTING ON...MOVING ON: ACCREDITATION AND PROGRESS   129

CHAPTER ELEVEN
STAFF DEVELOPMENT AND TRAINING   137

SUMMARY POINTS   147

APPENDIX A
REFERENCES/READING LIST   150
APPENDIX B
USEFUL ORGANISATIONS   155
APPENDIX C
THE DISABILITY DISCRIMINATION ACT 1995: FURTHER EDUCATION   157
APPENDIX D
CASE STUDY VISITS   159
APPENDIX E
THE QUESTIONNAIRE   160

ACKNOWLEDGEMENTS

Many thanks to all who were involved in the project. Margaret Chirico and Judith Rose were case study consultants and travelled hundreds of miles to interview staff and students. Without their invaluable help, the project would not have been possible. We are grateful to:

- the Local Government Association for its support
- the students whose experiences are quoted in this report, and who have spoken at conferences
- the many people who shared their ideas and experiences in writing and by telephone
- the colleges, local education authorities and Workers' Educational Association branches which were case study sites
- the project steering group members:

Tracey Austin, Sandwell College

Anne Baldwin, Ashworth Hospital

Georgina Clark, Mental Health Branch, NHS Executive Headquarters

Alison Cobb, MIND

Sophie Corlett, Skill

Liz Foster, Bolton Community Education

Richard Hooper, Lancashire Department of Education

Kathryn James, Clarendon College

Peter Lavender, FEFC

Viv Lindow, Consultant

Joy Mather, Mundella Community College, Leicester

Viv Parker, University of East London

Peter Raine, Consultant

Ruth Sagovsky, Peterborough District Hospital

Helen Wood, Sainsbury Centre of Mental Health

- project management on behalf of FEDA and NIACE:

Sally Faraday, Further Education Development Agency

Anna Reisenberger, Further Education Development Agency

Jeannie Sutcliffe, National Institute of Adult Continuing Education

Alan Tuckett, National Institute of Adult Continuing Education

- Steven Cull, the artist who did the painting used on the cover as part of a joint project between Pentreath Industries and Tate Gallery St Ives.

THE FEDA/NIACE PROJECT

To encourage and assist adult and further education providers to promote opportunities for learning, the Further Education Development Agency (FEDA) and the National Institute of Adult Continuing Education (NIACE) established a joint project. The Adult Learners and Mental Health project was set up:

- to carry out a national survey of continuing education for adults with mental health difficulties;
- to consider the implications of the NHS and Community Care Act and the Further and Higher Education Act;
- to identify key features of good practice in LEA and college provision;
- to investigate innovative approaches to meeting the learning needs of adults with mental health difficulties;
- to provide guidance to providers through a publication and conferences.

The project involved a national postal survey of all further education colleges and local education authorities in England and Wales. Two questionnaires were designed, one for FE colleges and the other for local education authorities (LEAs). They were completed in the summer of 1996, and 131 responses were received from FE colleges with 47 from LEAs. Where reference is made in the text to statistics, the percentages given refer to the percentage of responses to particular items. The project team also undertook case study visits to 21 sites with educational provision for people with mental health difficulties in England and Wales. Examples from the case study visits are referred to in the text to illustrate interesting or key points. Desk research identified other interesting and innovative initiatives.

This publication draws on all aspects of the project team's work and seeks to:

- describe the achievements of existing educational provision for adults with mental health difficulties;
- reflect the experiences of adult learners with mental health difficulties;
- demonstrate some of the different ways in which adult and further education for this group of learners can be developed;
- identify and discuss the range of issues which need to be addressed;
- identify those factors which appear to contribute to successful learning opportunities;
- highlight existing barriers to learning for adults with mental health difficulties;
- emphasise the central role of multi-agency working.

Who this publication is for

The project focused mainly on provision made by LEAs and further education colleges, but partnership with other organisations is a central theme and a key ingredient in developing successful learning opportunities for this group of adults.

Despite the fact that many of the issues discussed in subsequent chapters address directly the concerns of staff in education services, we hope that this publication will reach a wider audience including planners, policy-makers, managers and practitioners in education, health and social services. It is striking how often provision has been developed at the instigation of staff in mental health services or in the voluntary sector.

The report seeks to offer encouragement and guidance to those thinking about how they might develop learning opportunities for people with mental health difficulties. Hopefully it will also encourage those who have started off down that road but who are struggling with some aspects of their work.

Note: the terms 'mainstream' and 'discrete' are used in the publication, reflecting current practice of those in the field. Increasingly the more universal term 'inclusive learning' is being applied.

VOICES

Clarendon's project was aimed directly at people like me – people with mental health problems. Initial information was made so easily accessible to me. Clarendon's Education Counsellor, Kathryn James, met with the staff group at the day centre to describe the scheme; from there my key worker felt I could be a suitable 'candidate' and was able to give me enough information to allay some of my immediate doubts and fears, of which, following earlier experiences, there were quite a few!

Next the three of us met at the day centre for an informal chat. I have always regarded that meeting as a vital link in my progression towards college life. For a start, it felt important that Kathryn came to see me in my 'mental health' setting which I valued and she accepted me there.

Before the meeting I still thought it unlikely that college would have anything to offer me. By the end I had a package of information about a range of fascinating courses, a wide choice of opportunities tailored to my own interests and aspirations, a date for a follow-up discussion and arrangements for a guided tour of the college 'just to get a feel of the place'.

I recall that Kathryn wrote an instant summary of our discussions, with a copy for each of us to keep. That was particularly useful, not only as an aide-memoire but more significantly as a personal record of my aims and objectives and a tangible reminder of what I might be capable of achieving.

By then I was hooked. After a look around college I felt that the main site would be uncomfortably busy and I chose to enrol at one of the quieter learning centres where I felt immediately at ease. Having that option was invaluable in getting me off to a good start. Everyone there – tutors, staff and fellow students – were all so friendly and supportive that any anxieties or fears were quickly dispelled. It also helped that the course was solely for mental health service users with whom I felt able to be myself, on good days and bad.

JOHN

I'm married and have grown-up children and grandchildren. I used to work in a local factory where I was said to be a good worker. They were reasonably good about my mental health difficulties but then 'the change' started to affect by ability to cope. Eventually, after much coming and going and much heartsearching I took voluntary redundancy. I was getting more and more stressed and my problems with the work were affecting other people's bonuses.

I couldn't be left on my own and I couldn't go out on my own. I was terrified. I couldn't even put the washing in the machine, I know it sounds stupid but I couldn't even sort it out. My memory was affected too.

It's very difficult for people to understand something's wrong when they can't see something physically wrong. If someone can see a broken arm or leg they can sympathise but when it's going on in your mind…you feel so on your own. You think 'Am I making a fuss about nothing…or am I going mad?' You feel like you're on an island – in your own. They can't see the turmoil you're in.

Coming to the [ ] project was a real lifeline – something positive for me to do. I wanted something positive to help me get a grip on things again, something to work towards. The people round me all knew we had a problem of some kind but we were all trying to help ourselves. I didn't worry about the project [being for people with mental health problems]. I didn't think about that. It felt safe. They understood. I'm somewhere where people know there's a problem and I've got a chance to put things together again. Where I worked [before] it wasn't like that because they didn't know. They were plain ignorant. You felt an outcast really.

The tutors need to have a lot of patience and need to want to do that job. Some people really are poorly and find it hard to cope. It might help if other tutors know there's a bit of a problem.

I felt apprehensive about the work experience – dealing with people I didn't know. I used to get panic attacks but I'm better now.

The good things about [the project] are that I'm getting out and meeting people again; I'm with people prepared to help you if you try to help yourself. It makes me get up in the mornings; you can work at your pace.

[Now] I try to help. I feel people went out of their way to help me. I need to try and keep up with the course to show I'm grateful. And it's a way of putting something back into what I'm receiving.

JANE [name changed]

Before I started the courses I was a shy, introverted and anxious person. I wasn't very happy. The courses [on stress management and mental health awareness] have helped me to discover myself and to gain confidence. I feel empowered and it isn't just what I have learned about myself and about my own mental health. It's what I have learned about other people and the different ways of looking at mental health. Like now I know that I don't agree with the medical model and that the social model is much more relevant to me.

I don't have stars in my eyes, but I do believe I can do something to change things for people now. I have joined committees in the centre and we are campaigning for more staff and more activities. I am really proud of being part of making a difference. I want to help other people now.

There have been so many knock-on effects [of the courses], like the social skills you learn in the classes because you are talking with other people and getting more confident, and all the things that I do in the centre. Also I have been able to integrate the stress management into my everyday life and I am more focused.

The whole experience of learning has keyed me up for the future. I want to be a support worker. I believe I can do it. Eventually I'd like to be a counsellor but that's much longer term.
It's been like a personal revolution. It's been fantastic.

PETER (name changed)

It is years and years since I left school and I have wanted to return to education for a long time. I was frightened of failing and of not living up to expectations – my own expectations and what I felt were the expectations of others.

Eventually I felt brave enough to do some homework and I got some good marks which was a huge surprise, but very encouraging. I gained some confidence in my own ability and I'm pleased with my achievements.

I feel the most useful subject for me, to begin with, was study skills. Although the other classes very interesting, without going back to basics I don't feel I would have achieved as much as I have.

I have crossed over into mainstream college this term and in September I am going to do an access course. Next year I am going to go to university and after that, who knows?

SALLY

CHAPTER ONE

SETTING THE SCENE

Recent years have seen far-reaching changes in education. The Further and Higher Education Act of 1992 has significantly altered the way in which adult and further education services are funded and delivered, introducing major changes in the roles and responsibilities of colleges and local education authorities.

Alongside this, the 1990s have witnessed some of the most radical changes in health and social care (including services to people with mental health difficulties) since the birth of the welfare state in 1948. Long-stay hospitals are closing their doors – and not before time many would say.

But what does 'care in the community' offer instead? What part can adult and further education play in the lives of people with mental health difficulties?

A recent OFSTED review identified educational provision for people with mental health difficulties as a growing area of work, but as the Further Education Funding Council's Committee on Learning Difficulties and/or Disabilities (FEFC, 1996: 58-60) found, they are under-represented in further education. So while there are signs of increasing interest in developing provision, there is still a long way to go to ensure equitable representation.

The melting pot of change generates opportunity and threat. The closure of psychiatric hospitals has (in theory, if not always in practice) unlocked resources for community-based services including education and promises more humane and appropriate support but those moving into the community face an often hostile or at best fearful reception from their fellow citizens. The Further and Higher Education Act gave the Further Education Councils in England and Wales and the LEAs statutory duties to make 'adequate' or 'sufficient' provision for people with learning difficulties including those with mental health difficulties. With financial constraints leading to capped expenditure, student numbers are predicted to start falling in 1997. This gives rise to the concern that colleges may be discouraged from recruiting from under-represented groups, particularly if they have additional support needs.

INCLUSION: THE WAY AHEAD

We also have to recognise the inclusive role played by educational centres in the community...Drawing people into the community of learning is one of the most effective ways of tackling social exclusion.
KENNEDY, 1997

Education, as the recent major FEFC reports by Tomlinson and Kennedy (1996, 1997) have emphasised, is about more than promoting economic prosperity. The FEFC's Widening Participation Committee (FEFC, 1997) was very clear that participation in further education is also about achieving greater social cohesion:

equity dictates that all should have the opportunity to succeed.
KENNEDY, 1997: 3

Introducing his Committee's report (FEFC, 1996), Professor Tomlinson described the 'informing spirit' of their work: an 'inclusive learning' approach which focuses on:

the capacity of the educational institution to understand and respond to the individual learner's requirement...[and on] creating an appropriate learning environment.

If more people with mental health difficulties are to access education, colleges and local education authorities must not only develop inclusive learning approaches but become inclusive organisations. Introducing UNESCO's Salamanca

Statement on Special Needs Education (UNESCO, 1994), Federico Mayor described these as: 'institutions which include everybody, celebrate difference, support learning and respond to individual needs'.

One of the strengths of inclusion is its 'transferability' or applicability to other organisations – and to society at large. Inclusion is about enhancing the capacity of all organisations and communities to include those at risk of marginalisation and exclusion and to thus affirm that everyone belongs.

An inclusive approach recognises too that everyone has the potential to contribute positively to society regardless of their age, race, culture or disability. It can empower people traditionally disempowered and seen as dependent and passive recipients of help rather than as contributors to their community. As students with mental health difficulties in East Yorkshire discovered:

> *[The newsletter] is something we can hold up at the end of the day and show we've done something with our time...[it] makes me feel more worthwhile...putting something back, helping other people.*

> *I want to do a job but can't because of my condition. So I do something worthwhile for me, as well others. If I can help people with similar conditions, then I'm doing something worthwhile for myself as well. That's my main priority: to help others with mental health conditions. I enjoy it immensely.*
> QUOTED IN HUNTER, 1997

Inclusion, it must be emphasised, is not a crude interpretation of integration whereby anyone seen as 'different' is expected to conform to so-called 'normal' society and subjected to 'the tyranny of normality' (quoted in Wertheimer, 1997). Creating learning opportunities for people with mental health difficulties is not about sending people into mainstream classes without support and leaving them to sink or swim.

For some adults with mental health difficulties, an inclusive approach will mean ensuring that they have the necessary supports to use mainstream provision and enjoy a positive learning experience. For others it will involve the provision of discrete classes, enabling them to access continuing education on an equal basis with other adults.

TACKLING DISCRIMINATION

Principles are fine and good, but the real challenge lies in translating them into practice. A mission statement which sets out the college's or LEA's commitment to inclusion is a good starting point but strategic plans, equal opportunities policies, disability statements (required by the Disability Discrimination Act 1995) and other policies need to spell out clearly what steps the organisation is taking actively to encourage the enrolment of people currently under-represented amongst their users, including those with mental health difficulties.

The national postal survey, undertaken as part of this project, asked colleges and LEAs whether their strategic plans and disability statements (required by the Disability Discrimination Act 1995) specifically mentioned people with mental health difficulties. The replies were disappointing, although there was some evidence of future commitment to this area of work:

- Reference to people with mental health difficulties in strategic plans:
  Yes: 14 per cent   No: 86 per cent

- Planning to refer to people with mental health difficulties in future plans:
  Yes: 36 per cent   No: 64 per cent

- Reference to people with mental health difficulties in disability statement:
  Yes: 23 per cent   No: 77 per cent

It is also interesting to note how few organisations involve people with mental health difficulties in planning and drawing up their documentation. Our survey responses indicated that only one in five LEAs and one in 18 FE colleges do so.

People with mental health difficulties can experience discrimination in any aspect of their lives and education is not immune. A recent national survey by the mental health organisation, MIND, received 'reports of people being denied places on further education courses and professional training courses' (Read and Baker, 1996) and the experiences of this 49-year-old woman are not unique:

> *I was surprised to find a Head of Department art lecturer being so prejudiced. He said the college wouldn't consider taking on any other manic depressives and another lecturer said: 'It's all very well for doctors to tell you to go on college*

courses, they're not the ones who have to teach you.' I wonder how Van Gogh would have coped with such comments.
(READ AND BAKER, 1996)

The right to further and adult education was echoed by SKILL and eight other national organisations including MIND, in the Disabled Students' Charter, launched during the 1997 General Election campaign, which challenged the next Government to commit itself to lifetime entitlement to quality post-16 education for young people and adults with disabilities, including those with mental health problems.

Inclusive Learning (FEFC, 1996) also drew attention to developments in other countries where the right to education was promoted. In Australia, for example:

> *... appropriate provision for the inclusion of people who have or have had psychiatric disabilities [sic] is a basic human rights issue.*
> AUSTRALIAN GOVERNMENT PUBLISHING SERVICE, 1993

There remains the need to tackle the discriminatory practices identified by MIND (1996) and others.

IMPLICATIONS OF CURRENT POLICIES AND LEGISLATION

On 1 April 1993 the Further and Higher Education Act (1992) and (parts of) the NHS and Community Care Act (1990) came into force. Both have implications for people with mental health difficulties, and together with other policy initiatives such as the Health of the Nation (DoH, 1992), offer a sound basis for developing adult and further education provision at a local level.

Collaboration is a recurring theme throughout this book, and understanding the policy and legal context in which other services operate should be a pre-condition for working together. Staff in different agencies need to

- familiarise themselves with each other's agendas;
- understand the opportunities and constraints involved;
- identify commons aims and objectives; and
- form a shared agenda and a shared basis for moving forward.

Care in the Community

Under the government's Care in the Community programme (DoH, 1989), more people with mental health difficulties are being supported in the community. Those entering hospital are spending less time there and those who have spent many years in hospital are being resettled as long-stay hospitals close.

Education providers can expect increasing demand from people with mental health difficulties as long-stay hospitals reduce their bed numbers or close down and people are admitted to hospital for shorter periods. In Warrington, for example:

> *Strong links exist between the College and Winwick Hospital. The consultant there has identified 25 young adults who need educational provision in order for them to make a positive contribution to the community.*

Educational provision in the community, targeting people with mental health difficulties, can be a 'bridge' between hospital and community, particularly for those do not feel ready to move straight onto general (mainstream) classes. In York:

> *there was a particularly successful yoga class which was so appreciated by students that the [NHS] Trust decided to double the length of the course from 5 to 10 weeks. The students found it very relaxing. They wanted to know about classes where they could continue their learning when they left hospital and whether the WEA could provide another class in the community as most of them would probably find a mainstream yoga class too demanding.*

Changes in the way mental health services are delivered can be the catalyst for more widespread changes, including the development of more appropriate educational opportunities. In the East Riding of Yorkshire, for example:

> *Community Education's work with mental health services developed out of a traditional set of institutional classes in psychiatric hospitals – art, basketry, keep fit, etc. Research on hospital closure by the health authority pointed to the need for new educational opportunities in the community. The strategy adopted to move from the old to the new was to visit drop-ins and other places in the community and discuss possible classes with users and staff. Provision emerged from these discussions.*

With the increasing emphasis on collaborative approaches to planning community care, for groups as well as for individuals, colleges and LEAs need to ensure that education is on the agenda:

> *Specialist mental health and social care services… need to work closely with the agencies responsible for housing, income support, education, employment and training and leisure… purchasers… need to ensure that there is an effective partnership between the health and social care providers and other agencies such as housing, education…*
> (DOH, 1997: 3, 4)

The community care programme is based on principles which are consistent with the aims of education providers:

- services that respond flexibly and sensitively to the needs of individuals;
- services that allow a range of options;
- and services that intervene no more than is necessary to foster independence.

Although community care has opened up new learning opportunities for people with mental health difficulties in some parts of the country, it has also presented challenges.

- Education providers are increasingly having to compete with other services for funding.
- Funding of services to replace hospital provision is often inadequate, particularly for those needing more intensive support.
- The private health care sector is growing rapidly and providers often do not see a role for education nor are they always willing to fund it.
- With the introduction of purchaser-provider arrangements, joint planning forums may have less control over spending decisions.

> Private homes want an afternoon's entertainment for thirty people and they're not really prepared to pay for anything else.
>
> The future of our reminiscence sessions looks very bleak as the Trust's elderly mental health services are seriously overspent in this financial year and they will have to cut a further large amount next year. Budgets have been devolved to individual managers and education has to compete directly with physical care. The work we have been doing in partnership with health services for twenty years is increasingly under threat.

Health of the Nation

Health of the Nation (DoH, 1992) is a long-term Government strategy with the overall aim of improving the general health of the population. Prevention of illness and health promotion are seen as important and mental illness is one key area targeted for action.

Targets for mental illness include improving the health and social functioning of people with mental health difficulties and reducing the overall suicide rate.

Implementation of the strategy is seen as a shared responsibility on the basis that everyone can make a positive contribution to promoting health. The strategy has the support of all government departments and was overseen by a Ministerial Cabinet Committee.

Multi-agency initiatives or 'alliance working' is a central plank of the Health of the Nation strategy and to encourage collaboration the Department of Health makes annual Health Alliance awards. Lancashire County Council (LCC, 1997; Hooper, 1996) has developed a county-wide programme:

> *Lancashire County Council's Adult Education Service set up the Stepping Stones programme in 1993 to promote access to education by people with mental health difficulties. Since then, the enrolments by people with mental health difficulties have increased tenfold. Partners in the alliance include the county's adult education service, ten further education colleges, two adult education colleges, the county's Social Services Department, four health authorities and a number of voluntary organisations. In 1996, Stepping Stones won first prize in the Mental Health Category of the National Health Alliance awards.*

Further and Higher Education Act (1992)

The Act introduced far-reaching changes in the organisation and funding of further education. The reforms affect many different aspects of educational provision for people with mental health difficulties and are thus a recurring theme in this publication.

Central to the reforms was the establishment of the Further Education Funding Councils (FEFCs) for England and Wales which took over certain statutory duties previously the province of local authorities. Further education colleges were removed from local authority control and incorporated as independent institutions.

Under the Act, both the LEAs and the FEFCs are statutorily obliged to take account of the needs of students with 'learning difficulties' (including mental health difficulties).

FEFCs have a duty to fund and ensure the provision of courses under Schedule 2 including courses in independent living and communication skills, although funding is contingent on evidence of progression to other Schedule 2 courses. Provision is generally made in FE colleges

Local authorities, on the other hand, have a duty to fund and ensure provision of non-Schedule 2 courses. Local education authority adult, community education services generally make this provision. Also, some FE colleges provide LEA-funded non-Schedule 2 provision (and may also provide Schedule 2 courses, though they are not obliged to do so).

During the course of this project, a number of concerns were voiced by local providers. Generally these are discussed in other chapters but the most common issues are summarised below.

- With the incorporation of FE colleges, there is now no single forum for overall strategic planning of education for adults with learning difficulties. Local relationships between LEAs and colleges vary but in some areas links have been severed. The project also heard of cross-college links being severed since the introduction of the Act.
- The Act has generally boosted opportunities for vocational education but in many areas reductions in local authority financing of adult education has affected the provision of non-vocational education.
- Funding criteria do not always match the learning needs of people with mental health difficulties.
- Funding available for additional learner support does not always reflect the needs of people with mental health difficulties who may, for example, need extensive pre-enrolment guidance and assessment.
- The increasing emphasis on market principles in colleges has created a climate of competition. As a proportion of funding is attached to retention and achievement, these students may be less attractive to recruit.

But despite these difficulties, as the Tomlinson Committee pointed out in *Inclusive Learning*:

> *students with learning difficulties and/or disabilities are the only group of students specially mentioned [in the Act]. It not only places these students fully within the scope of further education, itself a powerful message, but also signifies the importance attached by government and Parliament to provision for them.*
> (FEFC, 1996: 4)

This report has also helped ensure that the needs of adult learners with mental health difficulties remain part of the national agenda for further education.

Responding to the consultation on *Inclusive Learning*, the FEFC (1997a) has announced that it is committing up to £1million to staff development. The Inclusive Learning Quality Initiative is a three-year centrally co-ordinated staff development programme. Groups of colleges will produce and pilot materials to improve the quality of inclusive learning. The materials will then be disseminated nationally.

The FEFC circular (1997a) also lists those recommendations from *Inclusive Learning* which are to be implemented now and announces the establishment of an Inclusive Learning Steering Group which will advise on this.

BENEFITS OF ADULT LEARNING

For anyone already making education provision for adults with mental health difficulties, the benefits are probably self-evident. The unswerving commitment of many staff and their belief in the value of the work are impressive. Nevertheless, provision across the country is patchy to say the least. Developing courses for mental health service users is not always seen as a priority or indeed as something worth developing.

Some education providers may not realise that people with mental health difficulties can benefit from learning opportunities. Staff in mental health services may also have no idea of the positive contribution which education can make to people's mental health.

REMIT, a community-college-based programme for people with long-term mental health difficulties in Leicester, carried out a survey of current project users in February 1996. One of the questions they asked was what people felt they needed from education. Responses indicate how educational opportunities can meet a number of different needs:

- Confidence: 32%
- Developing a new skill: 19%
- Academic qualifications: 16%
- Social contact: 13%
- Developing a new interest: 3%
- Other: 3%

The benefits will vary from person to person but during the course of this project there were many consistent messages about how participation in educational activities can have a positive effect on people's lives.

Learning new skills   In common with other adult learners, people with mental health difficulties can acquire new skills and knowledge. For some people this means being able to make up for lack of previous educational opportunities, perhaps because of emotional difficulties in childhood.

> The class was great, learning a new skill.
>
> It was nice to feel creative after telling myself I wasn't and never letting myself do crafts since the age of eleven.

Regaining former skills and abilities   For some people, access to education can also help them regain skills lost during periods of mental ill-health.

> I think I found some social skills again that I thought I'd lost. I spent so much time avoiding people in the past that I forgot how to communicate.

Increased confidence and self-esteem   For many students, a period of mental ill-health has shattered their self-esteem so to be in an environment where their views, skills and contributions are valued and where they can achieve something can have a very powerful effect:

> I was made to believe I was worth something and had a lot to offer.
>
> I feel a sense of personal achievement and the class has given me back my self-confidence and self-respect.
>
> I seem to be able to cope with just about anything now. I've gone so far forward in confidence that whatever happens I'm not going back. I've built up my self-esteem.

Feeling more empowered Having access to learning opportunities can help someone make the transition from disempowered patient to being a citizen with choices and rights:

> I now know I have the right to express opinions, make and refuse requests and give constructive criticisms.
>
> I feel I've more right to keep going at something…to do what I want to do …[and] not be so swamped by other people's needs.

Making friends and meeting new people Joining a class or doing a course can do much to overcome the isolation frequently experienced by people with mental health difficulties:

> The friendships were probably the most enjoyable aspect of my time at college.
>
> The most enjoyable thing about being at college was meeting new people I felt comfortable with.

Being viewed more positively by others This change of identity not only affects how people feel about themselves but also the way other people view them. Students may sometimes have a less than positive image but they are generally perceived as having more status than mental health service users:

> When I see my GP he says, 'Oh, you're at college', like you're doing something to get yourself on.

Structure and purpose to everyday life People who have been long-term users of mental health services can lose their motivation, ending up in a state of what is sometimes described as 'learned helplessness'. A course, or even a single weekly class, can help people begin to build some structure into their lives. The commitment to attend a class or course also provides a shape to the week:

> The most enjoyable thing about being on the course was having a meaningful daily occupation.
>
> The course gave me a sense of purpose in life.

A different identity Being a student allows a person to discard the identity of a 'patient' or 'client' and assume a more valued role. In an educational setting there are no diagnoses or psychiatric labels, no treatment, and no direct links to past mental health problems:

> At college I'm allowed to be a person in my own right.

The Psychology Department at St Ann's Haringey, which is involved with discrete provision for people with mental health difficulties at two local colleges, carried out an evaluation of some of these students (Lanham *et al*, 1997). Although only 18 students participated in the study (and there was no control group), the results are encouraging. They suggest net cost savings and likely long-term improvements in people's lifestyles:

- The number of days people spent as psychiatric in-patients was reduced by 85 per cent in their first year at college.
- Contact with psychiatrists and community psychiatric nurses reduced significantly.
- Students showed increased social confidence, communication and motivation, and their social networks increased.
- The majority were planning to continue in further education.

THE COSTS OF ILL-HEALTH

Mental ill-health is costly. It can cost people their jobs, their relationships and much else. Under-funded though mental health services might be, as the Tomlinson Committee points out in its report (1996) the costs of supporting people with mental health difficulties are high. If more educational opportunities were made available, not only would more people benefit personally, but the economic costs of mental illness might be reduced too. This is borne out by the research findings outlined above, which demonstrated savings to health and social care which exceeded the cost of college provision.

For some students, education can also be a route to employment, enabling them to become economically independent:

> *College is a more likely route to employment than for other people: college allows a person with mental health problems to develop the stamina and interpersonal skills needed for work. College is a demanding environment but more flexible and supportive than open employment. It also allows a person with mental health problems to gain the higher qualifications they will need to enter the job market at a higher level and sidestep the problems of an impoverished work or educational history.*
> (LITTLE, 1995)

Not everyone with mental health difficulties will end up in paid employment. Chronic or recurring mental health problems may make this an impossibility. But they can still benefit from opportunities for learning, opportunities which have often been denied them in the past as Chris Barchard, a mental health service user, reminds us:

> *Hospitals are full of under-achievers. Prolonged exposure to a culture where learning is not made possible and frequently not believed to be possible, makes people think that they cannot learn. People moving into supported accommodation need to benefit from the fresh start of community care. In every way a person can deteriorate in an institution and when out in the community again can start to recover from that experience. I am not saying that everyone is a Mozart because they have been in Park Prewett Hospital – but had he lived in our century that is where he might have been found!*
> (BARCHARD IN HAMPSHIRE COUNTY COUNCIL, 1994)

People with mental health difficulties are making it clear they want more education. A recent survey published by the Mental Health Foundation (1997) asked people who experienced periods of emotional distress about the strategies they used to take control of their lives. People had developed considerable expertise in finding ways of coping with their mental health difficulties and many felt that education had a part to play. The report of the survey recommended that:

> *local authorities [should] ensure equal access to sports and leisure facilities and adult education classes for people with mental health problems (for example, through training frontline staff, information to local statutory and voluntary mental health organisations, concessionary rates and targeted sessions.*
> (MENTAL HEALTH FOUNDATION, 1997: 9)

Given the importance attached to education, surely this is a mandate for developing more provision?

CURRENT PROVISION

From our national survey, case study visits, telephone interviews and informal networking activities, it is clear that an increasing number of colleges and local education authorities see this as a new and important area of work in the future, particularly in the light of the Tomlinson Committee's finding that people with mental health difficulties are an under-represented group in further and adult education (FEFC, 1996).

The survey asked colleges and LEAs to briefly describe what they saw as the unmet needs in relation to students with mental health difficulties. The following summarises their responses:

Outreach: lack of marketing strategies; groups not served by current provision including homeless people, minority ethnic communities and people with drug and/or alcohol problems.

Assessment and guidance: more time; suitably trained and qualified staff; ongoing post-enrolment guidance; appropriate pre-course assessment; better assessment frameworks; identification of emotional and social needs at assessment; ways of identifying difficulties during assessment; lack of expertise in counselling people with mental health difficulties; a less haphazard approach to assessment; more focused guidance and counselling.

Learner support: access to learner support assistants for non-Schedule 2 courses; mentoring and peer support; support into and on mainstream courses; support specifically for people with mental health difficulties; lack of social support; no 'on call' provision to deal with crises; shortage of learner support assistants; lack of support for people travelling to college; too few hours of additional tutor support; more flexible learning strategies.

Progression: support into employment; tracking people post-course; no support for students transferring to mainstream; no system for integrating students into mainstream provision; financial support for students on mainstream courses.

Staffing needs: more staff training around mental health issues; lack of training for support staff.

Evidence also emerged during the course of this project that a great deal was already happening, though people working in this area were often rather isolated from one another. SKILL's Mental Health Working Party, which has been meeting since 1991, has done a great deal to keep the issues alive and bring people together through conferences and other networking events. It is clear that being able to meet with colleagues involved in similar work is seen as valued, providing opportunities for information-sharing, mutual support and discussion of issues such as curriculum content.

Who is providing education?

Not everyone would agree with the psychiatrist in one hospital who declared 'We are all teachers here!' Nevertheless, it has been suggested that there is an educational component to many activities outside of formal education settings as Bee and Martin propose:

> *The first task, therefore, is to recognise the educational nature, latent or manifest, of mental health work. Adult education...is evident in the work of a range of agencies in the voluntary sector, informal community-based education, and, increasingly, in the more formal setting of further and higher education*

institutions. Often, however…no explicit reference is made to the 'education'
…even though the activities offered – such as creative writing, arts and crafts, dis-
cussion groups, personal development, computing and self-advocacy – are essen-
tially both educative and educational.

(BEE AND MARTIN, 1997: 128)

DIVERSITY OF PROVIDERS

Although the project has focused mainly on the work of colleges and LEAs, many others are also involved in the provision of education and training opportunities for people with mental health difficulties including:

- WEA (Workers' Educational Association);
- voluntary organisations (eg, MIND, Richmond Fellowship, National Schizophrenia Fellowship);
- NHS Trusts;
- vocational training schemes;
- industrial therapy and rehabilitation units.

DIVERSITY OF SETTINGS

Some classes take place on college sites or in adult education centres, but provision is also to be found in:

- day centres (social services, MIND, etc);
- day hospitals;
- psychiatric units in general hospitals;
- psychiatric hospitals;
- drop-in centres;
- community centres;
- special hospitals;
- NHS and private secure units;
- hostels and residential homes;
- centres for homeless people.

DIVERSITY OF PARTNERSHIPS

The most successful and flourishing initiatives we came across during the project all had a strong multi-agency focus to their work and is something we return to on numerous occasions in this publication when considering issues such as funding, access and guidance and progression. Partnerships included:

- an FE college and local MIND;
- an NHS Trust and FE college;
- a WEA branch and NHS Trust;
- an LEA and a drop-in centre;
- an Adult Education College, a voluntary organisation and Social Services.

DIVERSITY OF FUNDING

Current provision draws on a wide range of funding sources including:

- Further Education Funding Councils (England and Wales);
- Local Education Authorities;
- Joint Finance (NHS/LA);
- NHS (eg, for education in regional secure units)
- Mental Illness Specific Grant (MISG);
- Social Services main budgets.
- European Social Fund;
- City Challenge;
- Training and Enterprise Councils.

DIVERSITY OF PROVISION

Like other adult learners, people with mental health difficulties have diverse needs and aspirations. Existing provision includes:

- vocational and non-vocational provision;
- full-time and part-time courses;
- modular and non-modular courses;
- discrete and mainstream provision;
- taster courses, termly courses and longer courses;
- distance learning.

PLANS FOR THE FUTURE

Our national survey asked LEAs and colleges whether they were currently planning any new provision for people with mental health difficulties. Forty per cent
of respondents described a range of new initiatives which included:

- developing new partnerships with Trusts, local MIND groups, TECs and
  primary care teams;
- appointing specialist staff;
- new provision targeting specific groups (eg, young offenders, women,
  people in rural areas, GP referrals and adolescents);
- getting courses accredited (eg, through Open College Network);
- extending learner support (eg, setting up a befrienders' scheme and
  exploring ways of supporting people into mainstream provision);
- tackling progression, including finding work placements, setting up a
  taster course on access to higher education;
- developing forums for user involvement;
- looking at ways of increasing availability of current provision (eg, class
  size, timing of classes).

■ KEY THEMES AND ISSUES

- Care in the community has highlighted the potential role of education for adults with mental health difficulties.

- People with mental health difficulties are one of the three groups of under-represented learners highlighted by the *Inclusive Learning* report.

- Provision is currently patchy and under-developed on a national basis.

- There are pockets of provision where substantive work has been done.

- Partnership working is crucial in building educational provision for adults with mental health difficulties.

- Collaboration between agencies underpins much of the existing practice.

- Mission statements, equal opportunities policies and disability statements are a tool for change when converted to action.

- Only 14 per cent of survey respondents included mental health in strategic plans.

- There is diversity in the range of providers, the settings, the provision and the means of funding.

■ QUESTIONS

- What level of educational provision for adults with mental health difficulties is currently available in your local area?

- Who are (or could be) the key players across agencies?

- What are the strengths of existing provision, and what are the gaps?

- What steps would you need to take to address the gaps?

- Is education for adults with mental health difficulties cited as an integral part of:

    - ■ strategic plans?

    - ■ equal opportunities policies?

    - ■ community care plans?

CHAPTER TWO

WHICH LABEL?

The words used with reference to 'people with mental health difficulties' (the term used in this publication) are many and various. To try and ensure that respondents understood the focus of our work, we included the following information in the survey questionnaires we sent to colleges and LEAs:

> *The focus [of our survey] is adults who may be variously described as:*
> — *people with mental health difficulties*
> — *people with mental health problems*
> — *people living with (long-term) mental illness*
> — *people with a mental illness*
> — *mental health service users*
> — *people recovering from mental illness.*

A further, rather different, list was generated by participants at the expert seminar held at the start of the project and attended by a wide range of people:

> — *past and present (and future) users of mental health services*
> — *service user*
> — *recipient [of services]*
> — *patients*
> — *people with mental health problems (although they may not see mental health as their problem)*

> — *people who have difficulty with the learning environment*
> — *learners in an adult education world*
> — *people whose mental health is a barrier to learning*
> — *users.*

Although this publication uses the term 'people with mental health difficulties', these lists show that many different labels are in use. Some terms are strongly associated with mental health services and psychiatry, whereas others focus on mental health difficulties in the context of the learning environment. We return to this issue later in the chapter.

Labelling is not just a question of semantics. It has some important implications for this area of further education. During the course of the project a number of issues about labelling were raised by staff and students.

- Labels such as 'mentally ill' can attract stereotyped responses. For example, mental health difficulties may be equated with dangerous or violent behaviour

- Mental health difficulties may be confused with learning disability. As one person was told: 'You can't be mentally ill, you're too intelligent'!

- Some people may not enrol on a course for people with 'mental health difficulties', either because they don't wish to be labelled thus or they don't see themselves as having mental health difficulties.

- People with mental health difficulties may be 'otherwise labelled', often because of the services they use. For example: 'homeless', 'prisoner' or 'alcoholic'.

- Being called a 'learner' or 'student' is more positively viewed than being labelled 'a schizophrenic' or 'a manic depressive'.

- Labelling provision may attract funds from some sources which would otherwise be unavailable.

- If mental health difficulties are sensitively identified during the pre-enrolment advice and guidance sessions, arrangements can then be made to support people's learning.

- Labelling of some kind may be a good way in to reach some potential students. (We return to this issue in Chapter Six.)

A concern frequently mentioned by colleges and LEAs in their survey responses was that people with mental health difficulties were enrolling on mainstream courses but were not receiving support because they had not mentioned their mental health difficulties at enrolment:

> We possibly have many students with mental health difficulties who are receiving no formalised additional support. We do not do enough to encourage students to identify [mental health] needs.
> (LEA)

Although disclosure will not always be either appropriate or necessary, some people will have support needs arising from their mental health difficulties which can only be addressed if they are known to college staff.

The question of whether or not to label is discussed further in Chapter Six, but is mentioned here because it does say something about the negative and positive aspects of labelling.

There are no straightforward answers, but anyone making provision for people with mental health difficulties needs to consider the language and terminology they use and the messages the terms convey.

Providing for diversity

A large number of people will experience mental health difficulties at some point in their lives:

> *About one in four of the population consult their GP about a mental health prob-lem each year. About one person in seven has a diagnosable mental health problem (mainly depression and anxiety) in any given week.*
> (DOH, 1997A: 13)

Numbers alone cannot paint a picture of the diversity which education providers will need to consider. The various factors which need to be considered include age, previous education and previous history and all these will have implications for access, assessment, guidance, curriculum, learner support, and so on.

Age Mental health difficulties affect people of all ages. We came across colleges catering for young people who have been labelled 'school refusers', and classes for elderly people with dementia who had no contact with mental health services prior to the onset of their dementia. Much of the general 'mental health' discrete provision caters for people in their 30s, 40s and 50s, although one college told us that they had noticed an increasing demand for education from younger people.

Mental health 'history' Although much of the provision described in this publication caters for people who have had mental health difficulties for a number of years, some colleges and LEAs were working with students who had experienced a single episode of mental ill-health and were using education as a bridge to getting back into employment. Some people will have continuing mental health problems, though often interspersed with periods of 'wellness'. Some people will have spent many years in hospital, others will only have been admitted for brief periods.

Previous education People with mental health difficulties may have PhDs, or no formal qualifications, they may have difficulties with reading and writing. Some people may have developed mental health difficulties while still in their teens with the result that their schooling is likely to have been very disrupted.

Where people are living An increasing number of people will be living in their own homes or in supported accommodation in the community. Others will be living in hospitals, in secure units, in prisons, or in hostels for homeless people. Some will be living alone, others with their families and yet others in group living settings.

Severity of difficulties Some people will have mental health difficulties which dominate their lives and are a continuing source of distress. Others will never have used mental health services but may be at risk of developing mental ill-health and who perhaps approach or are referred to a college or adult education service at the suggestion of their GP or social worker.

Double jeopardy or double disadvantage

Many people with mental health difficulties are disadvantaged in terms of accessing education, employment and other opportunities. But some face 'double' or even 'triple disadvantage'. Two quotations from the MIND survey on discrimination (Read and Baker, 1996) highlight the need for services – including education – to recognise and work with diversity whether cultural, ethnic or religious. A 29-year-old man wrote:

> I suffer multiple discrimination: firstly on mental health grounds because of depression, secondly on being a single parent...and thirdly...[because of] my ethnicity.

And a 40-year old man diagnosed as having schizophrenia said:

> I suffer discrimination because of being held back all the time by other people who say it is my fault especially as I am from a West Indian background.

A number of respondents to our national survey were concerned about people who are sometimes described as having 'dual diagnosis: people with learning disabilities who also had mental health difficulties. Colleges and LEAs were often aware of a need to provide for this group but felt that their existing provision – whether for adults with learning disabilities or for those with mental health difficulties – was unsuitable:

> We are aware of an overlap, but uncertain how to respond.

Shared experiences

People with mental health difficulties are not a homogeneous group. Nevertheless they often share similar experiences of:

- isolation and marginalisation, without the network of family and friends which most people rely on for support and companionship.
- financial hardship – reliance on means-tested benefits, poor quality housing, inadequate income to pursue a decent lifestyle.
- lack of access to socially valued roles such as employee, student, friend, employer, contributor and so on.

- mobility – frequent changes of accommodation, sometimes because of going in and out of hospital.
- interrupted education and missed opportunities for training.
- unemployment, usually long-term or interrupted, even though some people may have worked for many years before developing mental health difficulties.

These kinds of experiences are well illustrated by students on a course in Leicester (Green, forthcoming):

> *A group of students on the LIFT course at Leicester Adult Education College were of different ages, came from diverse ethnic communities and there were many differences in their personalities, values, attitudes and experiences. However, they all:*
> - *were experiencing or had experienced mental health difficulties;*
> - *were living in rented accommodation in working class areas;*
> - *were living on means-tested benefits;*
> - *were feeling that appropriately paid and satisfying full-time work was the way to move out of their negative situation;*
> - *had left previous employment because of mental health difficulties;*
> - *had left school at fifteen.*

Access to further education can provide an opportunity for those previous experiences to be shared in a helpful way. It also offers the possibility of different experiences: a route to paid employment or other meaningful daytime activity; and the chance to make new friends. But collective learning by people with mental health difficulties can also provide an opportunity where these previous experiences can be shared and affirmed.

MENTAL HEATH DIFFICULTIES – DIFFICULTIES WITH LEARNING

Mental health problems can make it difficult for a person to learn. However, knowing someone's psychiatric diagnosis or label may not be much help in understanding their particular difficulties in learning. As research studies have shown (eg, Antony and Jansen, 1989, quoted in Little, 1995), medical labels are of little use in predicting how someone will cope in a learning environment:

as tutors we should worry less about the person's label and concentrate more on what we can see in terms of their behaviour and their ability, as well as what we can do to provide the most conducive environment for them.

(LEACH, 1996)

The remainder of this chapter describes some of the ways in which mental health difficulties may affect someone's ability to learn and cope with the learning environment.

The Open University has produced guidance on *Supporting Students with Specific Illnesses* (Open University, 1994: 23-26). However, written information should never be a substitute for finding out from individual students what they see as their potential difficulties or stresses. For anyone starting to develop provision, it is also worth remembering that:

- understanding someone's difficulties means you can start doing something to facilitate their learning;
- no one person is likely to have all the difficulties mentioned below;
- Students with mental health difficulties are not the only people who have difficulties with learning, but they may be more frequent and more intense.

Other chapters (especially Four and Nine) offer suggestions about how to tackle the issues raised here. Some barriers to learning will have a specific impact on how a student functions in the classroom but they also have implications for other aspects of provision including outreach work, advice, guidance and counselling services, arrangements for progression and accreditation and staff training and development.

LACK OF CONFIDENCE

For example:

- not wanting to enrol because you can't imagine you could get a place at college;
- fear of failure (not completing the course, not keeping up with other students, etc);
- expecting that previous bad educational experiences will be repeated;

- not feeling confident enough to approach anyone seen as a figure of authority, even if they are someone who could help you;
- problems with receiving feedback because it may be perceived as critical or negative rather than helpful;
- finding it difficult to initiate contact with tutors or other students;
- staying within safe limits rather than trying to move on;
- being withdrawn and isolated within the class.

> Guidance, counselling and support was essential to me . . . I needed the constant reassurance and feedback.
>
> I can't imagine myself saying 'No' . . . I've always done what others want. If I started saying 'No' I'd feel like someone else.
>
> I have a mental block for studying and homework – I hate it and resent time spent on it. Goes back to bad experiences at school and studying for 0 Levels.

LACKING ENERGY OR STAYING POWER

For example:

- difficulty in committing oneself to a course, particularly if it is longer than a few weeks;
- finding it difficult to get to classes, especially in the morning;
- tiredness and lethargy making it difficult to participate in classes;
- problems with time-keeping;
- irregular attendance and feeling unable to return after being absent;
- problems with meeting deadlines for assignments, etc;
- finding it hard to keep going through the day, because of general exhaustion.

> I spend most of the night trying to sleep. I force myself out of bed in the mornings and usually spend some time slumped in a chair with my eyes closed. I then spend the day trying to feel awake.

> It was very difficult to stick [to targets] at times – I lost my motivation, depression got in the way at times.
>
> I was enthusiastic at first [about college] but after coming down to earth, realised it might not be a good idea to take too much on because I feel lethargic a lot of the time.

ANXIETY

For example:

- feeling tense on arrival at college because the journey feels stressful;
- difficulty in coping with a busy environment such as a college campus;
- feeling too panicky to enter a room full of people;
- needing to leave the class suddenly;
- being too panicky to enter the canteen or any other noisy or crowded part of the building;
- difficulty with responding to verbal instructions;
- not being able to cope with changes such as tutor absence or a room change;
- unable to cope with any pressure.

CONCENTRATION AND MEMORY

For example:

- having a short attention span;
- not being able to remember what was learned the previous week or yesterday;
- being distracted by auditory hallucinations (hearing voices);
- obsessional thoughts making it hard to concentrate on learning tasks;
- difficulty focusing on several tasks;
- unable to tolerate interruptions;
- finding the environment over-stimulating (eg, too noisy or too crowded with people).

DECISION-MAKING

For example:

- not being able to decide whether to enrol on a class or course;
- taking a long time to reach a decision;
- difficulty in making choices because it feels like too much to be decided too quickly.

MOOD CHANGES

For example:

- public displays of emotion followed by embarrassment and unwillingness to rejoin the class;
- excitement and overtalkativeness so that other students avoid you.

> When I get a bit high...I feel very strong. I sleep four or five hours a night and feel far less hungry so start losing weight. I get a compulsion to talk, chattering to people in the supermarket or in the street under the slightest pretext. I get very optimistic, sometimes getting an urge to initiate exciting projects.

THE EFFECTS OF MEDICATION

The physical side-effects of prescribed medication vary from person to person but some will particularly affect the way a person functions in the learning environment. Common side-effects can include:

- restlessness;
- lethargy;
- thirst;
- increased frequency of urination;
- muscle spasms.

■ KEY THEMES AND ISSUES

- Adults with mental health difficulties can have a number of different labels. Some people do not want to attend 'labelled' provision.

- Mental health difficulties can affect adults of all ages and people from a wide range of educational backgrounds, from school leavers to postgraduates and older adults.

- Multiple discrimination is faced by some adults with mental health difficulties, for example people who are black, disabled or single parents as well as experiencing mental health difficulties.

- Medical labels are of little help in understanding how someone learns.

- Some adults with mental health difficulties *may* experience symptoms to include anxiety, lack of confidence, poor concentration/memory or mood changes.

- The side effects of medication *may* adversely affect learning.

■ QUESTIONS

- Which label(s) does your organisation use to describe adults with mental health difficulties?

- What labels do partner organisations and users prefer?

- Are they positive, negative or neutral?

- What age range of adults with mental health difficulties does (or could) your provision cater for?

- Is staff training available to help colleagues understand issues in relation to:

    - ■ labelling of people with mental health difficulties?

    - ■ the fact that mental health difficulties can affect anyone, regardless of age or educational backgrounds?

- Are students with mental health difficulties involved in designing and delivery of staff training?

CHAPTER THREE

PARTICIPATION AND EMPOWERMENT

We learn, when we respect the dignity of the people, that they cannot be denied the elementary right to participate fully in the solutions to their own problems. Self-respect arises only out of people who play an active role in solving their own crises and who are not helpless, passive, puppet-like recipients of private or public services.

To give people help while denying them a significant part in the action, contributes nothing to the development of the individual. In the deepest sense, it is not giving but taking – taking their dignity. Denial of the opportunity for participation is the denial of human dignity and democracy.

SAUL ALINSKY, RULES FOR RADICALS, 1971)

A t its worst, empowerment can be tokenistic: 'Tell us what you think, tell us what you'd like to happen, we'll even listen to you, but don't expect us to act on what you say'. The real challenge has always been to find ways in which education can truly empower people, both individually and collectively.

This chapter describes some of the ways in which adult and further education providers and students are already working in partnership. These examples could have been placed throughout this publication but the message might have got lost along the way.

By placing this chapter (and the following one) near the beginning, we also wanted to give a clear signal that participation is central and needs to be considered in every aspect of this work from initial planning through to evaluation.

Empowering people with mental health difficulties through learning opportunities is important because educational provision can:

- be a means of redressing the frequently disempowering effects of illness and treatment;
- offer an approach which is consistent with the overall aims of adult education (eg, shared learning between tutors and learners);
- challenge society's perceptions of people with mental health difficulties;
- contribute to a framework in which people can learn to take control over their own lives.

DEGREES OF 'EMPOWERMENT'?

Empowerment' tends to be used in a hopelessly rhetorical and sloganised way. What does it mean? What can education really do to empower people.

(BEE AND MARTIN, 1997: 129)

User or student participation in education can offer varying levels or degrees of consumer empowerment along a continuum:

——————/——————————/——————————/——————————————/——————————

Information   Consultation   Partnership   Delegated control

In the context of an education service for people with mental health difficulties this continuum could involve one or more of the following scenarios.

Information: publishing a leaflet telling people about the courses you are going to provide (ie, the provider has decided what needs to be provided).

Consultation: meeting with a local user group, telling them about your plans for the coming year and asking for their views (ie, listening to users though not necessarily being committed to acting on their views).

Partnership: a series of meetings between college staff and a local users group where they work out together how a new course will be run and what the content will be (ie, trying to decide together what new provision will be like).

User control: a local user group is paid by the college to set up and run a training course for college staff (ie, giving a group of people the resources and support to do things for themselves).

Whether as an education provider you decide to work in one or more of these ways, it is important to be clear about what you are doing. If as a specialist FE college worker you have decided to try and establish links with a local group of mental health service users, are you planning to ask their views on what you have already planned to do or are you really wanting to develop some kind of partnership?

From principles to practice

Some colleges and LEAs have addressed the issue of empowerment from the start in their statement of aims or philosophy on which provision is based. This makes sense because user participation is then integral and not something that gets tacked on. If it is not integral the danger is that it always drops to the bottom of the agenda – something that will be addressed when everything else has been sorted out. Dearne Valley College (with their local MIND group) wanted to establish a student-centred approach from the start which would be based on equal partnership between tutors and students:

> *The initial aims of the project were rooted in...a student-centred approach with continual negotiation with clients on the curriculum and content of the sessions, frequent reviews, small steps leading to an increase in self-confidence, self-esteem and as much user participation as possible. From an adult education perspective, it needed to be as close to a Freirean model as possible: a shared learning experience based on a relationship of trust between tutors and learners in an equal partnership...We saw the empowerment process as being crucial to the success of the project. We felt that it was in the level of user participation and partnership...that the learners would gain power and control over their learning.*
> (RUDDOCK AND WORRALL, 1997: 1)

Trusting users or students to find ways of empowering themselves is essential. Empowerment is not something that organisations bestow on others. As a mental health service manager points out:

> *Only where user-led initiatives meet up with the reformed hierarchy on a middle ground, where both are learning to share, do creative new shapes begin to form and influence the whole climate of service delivery.*
>
> (BATES, 1995: 41)

In Brighton, the South Downs Health (NHS) Trust has funded an education programme as part of its rehabilitation service for people with mental health difficulties. Providing a service which challenges the disempowerment experienced by users is central:

> *This service recognises the disempowering and demoralising effects of distress and service use...Users will be encouraged to take an active part in designing the courses, so that the content of the programme will be relevant to the participants' everyday lives and have practical application.*
>
> (GREATOREX ET AL, 1993)

Avoiding pitfalls

Developing user participation can be an exciting and rewarding journey for everyone and a great deal can be learnt along the way. But it needs careful preparation and planning.

Some colleges and LEAs have only recently begun to work with people with mental health difficulties, and others have not even started out, but experience of user participation in a few colleges and LEAs, as well as in other public services such as health and social care, provides some useful lessons for education.

- User participation will need proper resourcing; it requires investment of time, money and energy.
- Tokenism can easily creep in, even with the best of intentions.
- Everyone needs to be clear what is meant by participation so that everyone is working towards the same goals.
- Participation requires the support of senior managers and should not be seen as the sole responsibility of a junior member of staff.
- Real participation means recognising where existing power lies and redressing situations where people are unnecessarily disempowered.

At Clarendon College in Nottingham, students have a voice through membership of an Advisory Group and, more recently, in their own Student Forum:

> Students are represented on the Advisory Group for the Mental Health Support Service, alongside college staff and staff from mental health services. Student representatives are invited to attend on the basis that they will be able to cope with the Group's meetings and contribute on behalf of the students.
>
> The purpose of the Advisory Group is to inform good practice, but it has also been a valuable learning experience. Staff have gained greater insight into the support requirements for students with mental health difficulties and students and staff have been able to work out some of the boundaries to support (eg, what needs to be dealt with by mental health staff and how far the college supports, while remaining constructive and encouraging independence).
>
> A Student Forum has been established from the Advisory Group which is run by students and gives all students a voice. Issues are fed through to college management and have been dealt with.

It's important that everyone is clear who the 'users' are. It may seem obvious but professionals may see 'user consultation', for example, as asking carers for their views on services. Users and carers are distinct groups with their own perspectives and consultation with carers should not be a substitute for first-hand student involvement.

Sometimes even programmes which are set up with a clear user empowerment focus can be derailed as the following experience illustrates:

> The Learning Support Co-ordinator of a community education service attended a mental health conference with a user-colleague as the result of which they offered to set up a course to train users to advocate for patients in the local psychiatric hospital. The hospital insisted that each user must be paired with a carer. Users became disillusioned and now more carers are taking the training, leaving users feeling marginalised.

Planning and developing provision

Although the national survey indicated that people with mental health difficulties were rarely involved in contributing directly to strategic plans or disability statements, many colleges and LEAs had developed good links with local mental health user groups and day services. These contacts can serve a number of different purposes including: forging links between education services and users and finding out from users about the kind of courses they would be interested in and how and where these might be provided. In Southwark, this was done by commissioning a study (Gosling, 1994):

> The Southwark Day Care Forum, representing users and providers of community-based day care services, commissioned a study to ascertain the views of people with mental health difficulties about their educational needs. The study was jointly funded by Social Services (Mental Illness Specific Grant) and Southwark College. Current and previous mental health service users helped devise the survey. Two users were employed to work with the research consultant, helping design the interview schedule and piloting the questionnaire. They then interviewed the users, having been trained in interview techniques. The two users also contributed to subsequent presentations of the findings.

The Southwark project is one of a number of examples of ways in which users have been involved in planning provision.

- Students and professionals attending conferences together can be a shared learning experience, an opportunity to find out about what is going on elsewhere and to evaluate from different perspectives. Conference organisers could encourage attendance in pairs by offering free or subsidised places to users.
- The Speedwell Project is a rehabilitation project offering people with mental health problems opportunities to return to work or college. A Health Challenge grant enabled a staff member and a student representative to visit centres of excellence in the UK and USA to study ways of improving students' access and integration into education. The student also conducted research specifically into student/user perspectives and experiences.

- Mental health service users belonging to a working party which is drawing up college guidelines on students with mental health difficulties,
- The REMIT Users Group (RUG) at South Fields College, have been consulted by a working party (members include staff from REMIT, South Fields College, the Probation Service and the Regional Secure Unit) on risk assessment and management.

Asking potential students what kind of provision they want is only the starting point: a survey of user views, where day services staff and tutors were also interviewed, provided some interesting if rather conflicting views!

> When users were asked if gardening would be of interest, a clear majority said no. Day centre staff, on the other hand, were highly enthusiastic: 'wonderful...so therapeutic... opens up so many avenues...'

Asking people what they want to learn makes sense, but how many colleges and LEAs have reached the point where involving users in programme planning is seen as essential and natural? It could mean re-shaping provision quite substantially. College programmes may have remained unchanged for a number of years because 'that's what we've always done and it seems to work...' but it may be founded on what other people have decided is best for students with mental health difficulties. Long-term illness, lack of self-confidence, being treated as dependent and in need of care can produce rather acquiescent students. Enabling students to express their wishes may in itself be a significant challenge.

AN EMPOWERING CURRICULUM

For some people, getting to college for the first time will be a major achievement: empowerment can start with walking through the door.

Learning opportunities can be empowering both individually and collectively for people with mental health difficulties. The content of courses and the way students learn and are taught can all help people feel more in control of their lives, more confident, more able to take decisions and generally develop a lifestyle of their choice.

Much of the provision designed specifically for people with mental health difficulties includes classes which have a clear focus on empowering individuals through personal development. For example:

- Assertiveness
- Social Skills
- Communications
- Self-Advocacy
- Budgeting
- Confidence Building
- Life Skills
- Improve Your Image
- Stress Management
- Reading and Writing

Alongside this kind of provision, where the main focus is on individual learners, an increasing number of providers are developing opportunities for collective development, sometimes working together with existing user or self-help groups. The Community Education Service in East Yorkshire promotes and supports self-help groups in various ways including:

- deploying an IT tutor to work with a group of users to produce a newsletter;
- preparing an evaluative account of groups, emphasising personal and collective outcomes;
- enabling students from two self-help groups to attend a groupwork skills course;
- together with MIND and Social Services, running workshops on welfare rights.

For many learners with mental health difficulties, one of the most important aspects of discrete provision is the opportunity to be part of a group of people who have much in common. Talking or writing about these shared experiences, in a non-judgemental and supportive environment, can be an affirming and empowering experience as these students found in a creative writing group:

> *There was a great deal of discussion on topics chosen and it became clear that some of the discussions were a form of group therapy. The most outstanding example was when a member of the group who suffered from severe depression wrote his first poem… Other members quickly identified with his feelings and it opened up a discussion on depression and on what it actually meant.*

(RUDDOCK AND WORRALL, 1997)

Lewisham Community Education Service has been working with a group of people with mental health difficulties at the Independents Day Centre:

> The students have been recording their past experiences through the medium of photography in a project designed to maximise user control. The group has produced a photographic record of the closure of a local hospital (where most of them have been in-patients in the past). Their work was displayed in the Town Hall at the Mental Health Trust Fair. The group is currently negotiating with the Trust who wish to purchase poster-size copies of the photographs. Income from the sales will belong to the group who will decide how it will be spent.

User participation in outreach

Current students with mental health difficulties often act as informal role models for others who may be thinking about whether to join a class but are unsure whether this is something they will be able to do. Seeing people who share similar difficulties already at college can be a powerful incentive: 'If they can do it, maybe I can too.'

This kind of informal outreach is a very effective recruitment tool, but existing students can be involved in outreach and marketing in more structured ways too, as the following examples demonstrate:

- Using quotations from students on posters, leaflets, brochures and other publicity material.
- Featuring students with mental health difficulties on videos about provision.
- Groups of students visiting local mental health drop-ins, day centres and other places where they can meet and talk to potential users of adult education services.
- Displaying students' work such as photographs, paintings, poetry and other creative writing.
- Users/students helping to run an introductory afternoon of taster sessions for people thinking of joining classes.
- Being involved in writing an induction leaflet for new students with mental health difficulties.

User participation in quality assurance

Introducing the *Inclusive Learning* report, Professor Tomlinson stated the Committee had found:

> *clear evidence that the quality of provision made for these students [with learning difficulties and/or disabilities] is less good than that to be found in colleges generally.*
> (FEFC, 1996: 6)

To rectify this, the report makes substantial recommendations on quality assurance, suggesting that:

> *opportunities for students to say what they want from colleges are a fundamental element of good quality assurance arrangements.*
> (FEFC, 1996: PARA 10.20)

All students should be able to participate in quality assurance procedures, but for learners with mental health difficulties it can be particularly important. It demonstrates the organisation's commitment to empowering people with mental health difficulties. In some cases, it may be the first time they have been asked for their views on a service they are using.

For organisations starting to run courses for people with mental health difficulties, students' feedback can be used to inform the way provision develops subsequently. The LIFT Project at Leicester Adult Education College aims to help people with mental health difficulties get (back) into paid employment:

> The project co-ordinator undertook a detailed survey (Green, forthcoming) at the end of the first year and the findings were used to shape recommendations on how the project should develop in future. Students completed an evaluation form which provided both quantitative and qualitative data about all aspects of the project including guidance and support which are a key element of LIFT.

Questionnaire surveys can be a relatively straightforward way of collecting information and for some students may be less daunting than being asked for verbal feedback in a group or in one-to-one interviews. However, careful attention must be paid to how questionnaire surveys are devised and carried out. For example:

- are students involved in drawing up the questions?
- can students support one another to complete the questionnaire?
- are students invited to help analyse the results?

The REMIT project for people with long-term mental health difficulties wanted to ask users whether the project was meeting their needs:

> A questionnaire was delivered over 4 weeks to a cross-section of users. The majority of questionnaires were delivered by users, supporting each other to fill out the respondents' details. The collating of results was carried out by a staff member and a user working together. The results were used to shape future developments in REMIT.

Inviting an external consultant to meet students is another way in which organisations can get useful feedback from students:

> The Education Programme in Brighton run by South Downs NHS Trust uses a range of 'quality checks' including the employment of an outside consultant. The consultant meets twice with students on the Main Course and once with students on the Pre-Course and Post-(Main) Course. After the discussions, the consultant goes over the points raised and students decide what is to be fed back to the Programme's steering group.

Inclusive Learning drew attention to the 'inadequate variety of ways of [students] making their views known' (FEFC, 1996: 159). Standard approaches to gathering information are not always appropriate and alternative methodologies may be needed, as Lancashire's Adult Education has discovered:

> The New Directions (Mental Health) Programme at the Adult College Lancaster has been working with the Responsive College Unit (RCU) developing a methodology for evaluating the Programme. The RCU's objectives include reporting on students' perceptions of the effectiveness of current courses. One method being considered is holding focus groups for students, although one-to-one interviews are also being tested out.

As Lancashire's experiences demonstrate, there is a need to experiment with a range of approaches to evaluation. In the East Riding of Yorkshire, the Community Education Service's adult education organiser (mental health) developed a biographical approach with mental health service user groups:

> *A biographical approach...placed students in the driving seat, offering them a degree of control of the process...I felt the exercise would enhance my understanding of the experiences and interests of those whose learning I sought to plan and facilitate.*
> (HUNTER, 1997: 212)

User participation in staff development and training

Colleges and LEAs are beginning to involve people with mental health difficulties in staff training and development. Users who can talk directly about their experiences and help staff think about how they can support people more effectively make an invaluable contribution:

> At Mathew Bolton College, Birmingham, staff training has been provided by a user group with European Community funding.
>
> At Clarendon College, Nottingham, mental health awareness training is delivered by service users and providers working together. Users have also been involved in staff development sessions targeted at specific groups such as college reception staff.

Education providers can also be involved in 'training for trainers'. There is an established need for mental health service users to provide training or other inputs such as advice and consultancy to education – as well as health and social care – providers. The recently completed National User Project, funded by the NHS Executive (Lindow, 1996), and other initiatives such as the Citizen Involvement Project (Beresford and Croft, 1993) are enabling more people with disabilities to work as trainers and consultants. Courses on public speaking, for example, can help users develop the skills needed for consultancy and training work. Providing training of this kind can be a good way of supporting local user groups and enabling a larger number of people to become trainers and consultants.

The user movement developed in the 1980s in response to the lack of empowerment, freedom and choice in mental health services, although dissatisfaction with psychiatry has a much longer history. The challenge for education providers is to work in collaboration with user groups, to listen and learn from what they are saying. Learning must be a shared two-way process.

Thanet MIND and Thanet College have been running a one-year training course for mental health service users:

> The aim of the User Consultancy/Empowerment Training was to develop personal and presentation skills, including use of materials and equipment, and enable the students/users to make well prepared and professional presentations to groups of professionals and students. The content of the first course was negotiated with the students. Initially intended to be part of a day each week, sessions were extended to a whole day as additions were made to the content of the course.
>
> Information about local service agencies gave students an understanding and overview of service delivery. Sessions on diagnoses and treatments were supported by a counsellor who offered group and individual support. This was necessary because of the nature of the students' unresolved difficulties and became a well-used resource.
>
> Students gained different things from the course including new skills and increased confidence and self-esteem. Some were hoping to form a consultancy group. Several planned to do the City and Guilds (7036) Teaching Adults course.
>
> After two years, funding was no longer available, but Thanet MIND are planning to take the course to colleges in other areas.

This chapter has looked at how students with mental health difficulties can be involved in all aspects of educational provision in ways which are genuinely empowering. The next chapter continues this theme, exploring how educational opportunities can be developed to reflect and maximise student-centred learning.

KEY THEMES AND ISSUES

- Learning can offer real chances for empowerment and participation for people with mental health difficulties.

- User participation needs time, energy and money.

- People with mental health difficulties can get involved in a number of ways – such as planning provision, being on working parties and offering training.

- The curriculum can offer opportunities for personal development/empowerment by including topics such as confidence building, communication skills and public speaking.

- Students with mental health difficulties can play a role in outreach/marketing of courses.

- The views of users are essential in evaluation and monitoring of quality.

QUESTIONS

- What opportunities does your provision offer for students with mental health difficulties to develop self advocacy skills and to be represented in your college/adult education centre?

- Are there opportunities for people with mental health difficulties to sit on student committees, working groups etc?

- Does your curriculum offer include topics to support personal development/empowerment?

- Can resources be allocated to support students with mental health difficulties to take an active role in training and quality initiatives?

CHAPTER FOUR

OVERCOMING BARRIERS TO SUCCESSFUL LEARNING

The barriers which prevent people with mental health difficulties from accessing and using adult education provision may relate to personal factors such as lack of confidence, poor motivation, low income, or difficulties with travelling. But there are organisational barriers too: inadequate advice and guidance pre- and post-enrolment; insufficient resources for classroom support; or an overly narrow curriculum.

A closer look reveals that barriers are wide-ranging and include:

- lack of information about what is or may be made available;
- difficulty meeting the costs of transport and fees;
- transport problems;
- negative attitudes of staff and other students;
- failure to identify and provide for learning support requirements;
- large and busy campuses;
- emotional barriers;
- timetabling of courses;
- funding criteria.

Overcoming these and other barriers will have implications for all aspects of provision for people with mental health difficulties including outreach, marketing, assessment and guidance, learner support, curriculum design and delivery, progression, etc. Some barriers will be more difficult to overcome than others. For example, it is probably relatively easy to hold classes at a time of day when people are best able to learn; it may be more difficult to find a venue which students don't find too intimidating.

The remainder of this chapter has a series of headings which describe some broad themes or 'core conditions' that we believe need to be addressed if people are to have successful learning experiences:

- diversity of provision;
- consistency and continuity;
- flexibility;
- a welcoming environment;
- respect;
- expectations;
- achievement.

These 'core conditions' apply to all adult learners and, if embedded in provision for students with mental health difficulties, should help to improve the learning environment for everyone.

Diversity of provision

As earlier chapters indicated, people's mental health difficulties are very diverse, leading to different learning and support needs. To accommodate diversity, can providers offer:

- a range of provision, including opportunities for people to learn to-gether or to join and be supported in any learning programme?
- a choice of vocational and non-vocational courses or a combination of both?
- a range of courses able to cater for people with little previous formal education who may need access to basic literacy and numeracy classes as well as for people who have completed university degree courses?
- courses for people wanting to enter or re-enter paid employment, people wanting to find voluntary work and those who have no clearly defined goals at present?

- provision in off-site settings such as day centres or community locations as well as in college buildings or other mainstream education premises?
- flexibility of provision which can cater for people in different states of wellness, including those at risk of developing mental health difficulties as well as people with chronic or long-term mental ill-health?
- courses for people with a range of mental health difficulties as well as provision targeting people with particular needs such as elderly people with dementias; homeless people or people from minority ethnic communities (see Chapter Five)?

A broad curriculum has been developed by Barnet College:

> The Community Link Course is a one-year course for people recovering from mental health problems who want to increase their confidence, participate in the local community and develop useful and creative skills. Subjects vary from year to year, depending on the individual students' interests. In one year they included:
>
> | | |
> |---|---|
> | – individual and group tutorials | – women's issues |
> | – arts and crafts | – communication |
> | – current affairs | – computing |
> | – English workshop | – drama |
> | – food studies | – health studies |
> | – improve your image | – looking ahead |
> | – jazz dance for women | – maths workshop |
> | – photography and ceramics | – printing plus |
> | – music | – sport |
> | – yoga | – issues for men |

Consistency and continuity

Learning to cope with changes may be important for some people with mental health difficulties, but providing a sense of continuity and consistency, particularly for new students, will be essential if they are to develop confidence and trust. The kind of things which experienced providers have identified as important include:

a clearly identified person: so that students can put a name to a face, and have someone with whom they can build up a relationship of trust over time. Familiar faces are important.

consistent venue: being moved from room to room every week, or finding there's a sudden room change one day, can be very difficult for students to handle. This can be seen as a minor irritation by staff, but can be very upsetting for students.

consistent staffing: tutor absences are sometimes unavoidable but need to be kept to a minimum. Wherever possible, a substitute tutor should be someone already known to the students.

reliability: keeping appointments and being generally reliable not only shows respect to students but gives a clear message that the service is reliable and consistent.

link provision: moving an off-site class onto a college site so that students start at college with a tutor they already know.

> I think what is crucial is that [the students] establish links with at least one person they know…that they have met someone in an environment where they feel comfortable so that when they come to college they know someone there; then if they feel anxious during the day at least they have someone in college [to whom] they can say 'Look, I can't go back to my class'…so they don't just fly out of the college and then worry about coming back. (Student)
>
> Consistency of tutor staff is very important. I'm very hot on this. I'll do my best to get another tutor if someone 'phones in but it's really important to keep it the same. That security is important. (Course organiser)

Offering continuity within a system which has term-times and breaks can be difficult but may be very important for some students for whom the holiday breaks can be very hard to handle. The long summer holidays can leave some students feeling very vulnerable. Bournemouth and Poole College managed to find a way round this:

> The college has been running a programme for students with mental health difficulties since 1993. Terms have now been reorganised with four ten-week terms and breaks of only three weeks.

When breaks do occur, it is necessary to prepare students well in advance and to avoid the feeling that it has been sprung upon them. Similar preparation needs to be made for the end of a class, course or learning programme.

Flexibility

If a flexible approach can be built into all aspects of the work from the start it can significantly reduce the chances of people dropping out.

Here are some of the strategies which people have adopted to make their service more flexible and responsive to the particular needs of people with mental health difficulties:

- Allowing for 'open absence' during periods of ill-health, recognising that 'interrupted learning' will be inevitable for some people.
- Allowing for the fact that students may need time off for hospital or other appointments.
- Offering a programme each week within which students can make choices and share activities, rather than expecting them to make a choice which has to be followed for a whole term.
- An enrolment system that enables people to join a class or course at any point during the year.
- Mix 'n match courses so that people can attend part or all of a course and also have a choice of subjects.
- A modular curriculum and flexible learning opportunities so that people can have breaks in learning if they need to.
- Offering students the chance to try out a mainstream class while still on a discrete course so they can test the water before leaving, the more supportive environment of discrete provision.
- Being prepared to schedule classes at times of day when people are more

likely to attend and be able to learn such as the middle of the day and during the afternoon ('good timing').

- • Courses which identify learning styles and use different teaching and learning strategies to accommodate students' different preferences.

> What you need in terms of an education structure is to be able to drop out until it's over and then drop back in. In a way it would need to be modular. So you're not trying to catch up, whether it's three or four weeks that you've missed. [If] it's all in modules...you get as far as you get and get accredited for that...and so on... you're still working for a formal qualification.'

A welcoming environment

For people with mental health difficulties, the prospect of entering a busy college building can be very frightening – so daunting that they may not even get as far as enrolling. It can be easy to overlook or underestimate the scale of the barriers posed by the physical environment. Creating a welcoming environment really matters as these comments illustrate.

> The move from the Centre to the college itself was difficult. Actually walking into college was a huge ordeal. One student said he still had to take a deep breath before coming through the entrance, which is always busy. Nobody chose to use the main refectory because of the noise and bustle.
>
> It remains difficult to create a user-friendly environment in a building which has many unfriendly features: tower block, small lift, long corridors, narrow corridors.
>
> The community college has the problems of a typical secondary school building – long corridors, for example, which some students find scary.

A building cannot easily be rebuilt or adapted but a welcoming atmosphere can help to compensate for physical barriers:

The Bolton Community Education Service is based in a typical adult college building. Physical access is a problem, but it is friendly, unthreatening and welcoming. It is easy to see why the centre is favoured by people with mental health problems and by the agencies which support them. The staff are part of this welcoming environment; there's a good sense of mutual respect and warmth.

The atmosphere in a building reflects the culture and values of the organisation which cannot be changed overnight. But if an organisation is committed to extending its provision to serve under-represented groups, including people with mental health difficulties, creating an environment which offers a positive welcome will be essential.

Meanwhile, here are some specific ways in which education providers are trying to create a more welcoming and safe environment for people with mental health difficulties.

- Providing mental health awareness training for frontline staff such as receptionists, security personnel and library staff.
- Using befrienders who can travel to classes with a student or meet them at college and accompany them to the door of the classroom.
- Arranging for students to use the canteen at less busy times or for a group to go there together.
- Making signposting clearer so that students do not have to keep asking people for directions.
- Arranging for new students to visit the college campus during quieter or holiday periods before they start so they can begin to familiarise themselves with the building.
- Pairing up students on the same course and going to college together so that they can support each other.
- Organising an identified place that feels 'safe' where students can meet before and after class.
- Moving a class which has started in off-site provision such as a day centre onto a college site, so that students enter a potentially threatening environment as part of a group who already know each other.

As one student commented:

> *Not only have I had to overcome my own personal barriers, but also those of people's attitudes and beliefs about mental illness…At times I have felt very isolated and alienated by my environment.*
> (DEFFLEY, 1996)

Going to a class for the first time can be daunting but it can also be the first of many new achievements, as this student on a creative writing course wrote:

> Friday came, it was time to go.
> Butterflies in my stomach and a very dry throat
> I climbed up the stairs…opened the door…
> it was my first step, I made it on my own.

Respect

Low self-esteem and lack of self-confidence are common amongst people with mental health difficulties. The stigma of mental illness, negative public attitudes and the experience of using psychiatric services all contribute to these feelings. Learning opportunities can encourage feelings of self-worth and self-respect.

- Being treated as students by tutors and other staff rather than as 'patients' or 'clients'.
- Tutors who are respectful and supportive without being patronising.
- Training for reception and administrative staff which ensures that all students are treated respectfully and in a positive manner.
- Having written and other information about provision for people with mental health difficulties which gives clear messages that this is seen as an important and worthwhile area of work
- Respecting people's abilities (while acknowledging disabilities) so that students take some responsibility for themselves rather than reinforcing the dependency culture which can operate in mental health services.

Staff who are respectful to students and value them as people are highly regarded as these comments illustrate:

Staff treated you as people…staff listened to you and they remembered what you had wanted to do…no one told you off automatically…the staff were prepared to talk to you about anything…no false accusations were made about students.
GREATOREX ET AL, 1993

The most senior health professional interviewed spoke of [the educational staff's] respectful style of relating to students…students saw education staff as less directive than health board staff.
MAIN, 1996

Expectations

Time-limited, structured courses…can enable [people] to develop skills, learn new ones and grow in confidence and independence. This challenges traditional day services for [people with mental health difficulties] which have tended to be low-key, drop-in and open ended with an expectation of maintenance rather than rehabilitation… [on these courses] the environment is one of a relaxed expectation that students will study.
GREATOREX ET AL, 1993

Motivating potential students can be difficult, particularly if they have spent many years in hospital or been using day services where little may have been expected of them in terms of progress or achievement.

In some cases, pressure at work or in other areas of their life may have triggered their mental health difficulties so that any situation where they feel under pressure can be very threatening.

If there are clear messages that students will not be put under any pressure to achieve, this can play into students' low expectations of themselves; but if, on the other hand, they are told they will have to leave if absent for more than a certain number of weeks, some may not even enrol. Finding the right balance for each student is important.

Carrots are generally preferable to sticks and encouragement is welcomed by many students. The concept of 'a relaxed expectation that students will study' referred to above strikes a balance, as two students explained:

> You need a breathing space. You're making a big move from somewhere – hospital, or day centre – to college. That's enough in itself. You need to be able to come and say what you're doing and nobody's going to worry me. I'll just sit in the classroom and enjoy it. Up to a year, maybe for more than a year, there'll be no pressure.
>
> Nobody told me 'You must do this and you must do that' but through not having too much pressure and not having to achieve this, that and the other I actually worked well anyway and got on...but if somebody starts saying 'You've got to do this, you must achieve that', then I'll go down.

Not everyone joins a course with low expectations. Students may assume that they will return to their previous employment or get a similar job. For some people, going on a course may lead to a realisation that if they do return to work, it will be to a less demanding job. Others may go on a course designed to help people think about work as a future possibility but have to revise their ideas, as these students found (quoted in Green, forthcoming):

> Very frustrating knowing the bottom line, eg, I can only do fairly 'low paid' jobs – not enough education.
>
> I seem to be 'qualified for the wrong jobs for me', and not qualified enough for more enjoyable and better paid work.

The continuing availability of advice, counselling and general support can help students develop realistic expectations about future options such as employment.

Achievement

Failure is familiar to many people with mental health difficulties. The very fact that they have become 'ill' may be experienced as a 'failure to cope'. So minimising the possibility of failure and marking achievement is important:

> *...the psychological impact of failure is greater on someone with arguably lower self-esteem, self-confidence and a poorer self-concept as a learner... [a study of supported education found that] although these students' drop-out rate was not*

perceived to differ greatly from that of the general student population . . . [the] impact was greater.
LITTLE, 1995: 4

. . . they should say, 'You're good at that. And maybe you could do that as a living or as a hobby . . . I mean there's often things they could say . . . just little things that would help.
GOSLING, 1994

Achievement is often measured in terms of specific outcomes successful completion of an assignment, achieving a qualification, passing an exam – but for some students with mental health difficulties, getting up in the morning and getting themselves to a class is a major achievement which needs to be recognised as such:

It is particularly important for students and staff to record and celebrate achievement at whatever level and in whatever form.
OPEN UNIVERSITY, 1994: 5

■ KEY THEMES AND ISSUES

- There are a number of major barriers to education for adults with mental health difficulties – from negative attitudes to lack of appropriate learning support.

- Core conditions for success are:

  - ■ a flexible, diverse range of learning opportunities

  - ■ consistency/continuity eg of staff/venue

  - ■ a welcoming adult environment

  - ■ respect for students with mental health difficulties

  - ■ positive expectations without pressure

  - ■ a sense of achievement for students, not necessarily defined in terms of vertical progression.

■ QUESTIONS

- What barriers can you identify to participation by adults with mental health difficulties?

- What barriers do people with mental health difficulties themselves identify?

- What solutions are possible?

- Do you offer:

  - ■ a wide range of provision?

  - ■ consistency of staffing/venue?

  - ■ a welcoming environment?

  - ■ support without pressure?

  - ■ a chance for students to define their own targets / achievements?

- Is provision flexible enough for students to stop and start again, if illness interrupts their learning? (People may need several attempts to do a course).

CHAPTER FIVE

MAKING IT HAPPEN

As the Tomlinson Committee (FEFC, 1996) asked: what are the factors that determine whether under-represented groups such as people with mental health difficulties get to participate in further and adult education? Or to put it slightly differently: how do things get going and who or what ensures continuing growth and development?

GETTING STARTED

The catalysts are often a combination of 'people, policies and pounds'. There are many different routes to establishing provision for people with mental health difficulties, as these examples, identified during the course of the project, show:

- The local psychiatric hospital asked the FE college in their area to establish provision for people leaving hospital and made some funding available for this.
- An LEA which had traditionally provided classes in hospitals was asked to develop provision in the community for ex-residents.
- A college identified a need for specialist provision for people with mental health difficulties who were attending ESOL classes.
- An influential member of the local community, whose son had mental health difficulties, became a strong advocate for establishing provision

which led to classes being set up.

- Staff working in adult education and mental health services jointly identified the need for specialist provision.
- Day service providers, who were exploring ways of extending the range of day opportunities beyond traditional day care provision, asked their LEA to run some classes.
- A senior LEA officer, strongly committed to developing provision for people with mental health difficulties, was instrumental in developing a county-wide strategy and securing funding.
- Successful provision by one college raised the profile of this work which led other colleges in the area to develop provision too.
- A MIND group approached their local college and suggested that they worked together to develop courses.

A designated staff post

The national survey asked colleges and LEAs if they had a designated member of staff responsible for students with mental health difficulties. Less than half did. Those colleges and LEAs which were struggling to meet the needs of students with mental health difficulties recognised this lack of a designated staff member with appropriate expertise as a reason for the lack of development of provision, as some of the survey responses indicated:

> We have no named person with specific expertise.
>
> …no person to specifically look at this and develop this area properly.

Having at least one staff member with specific responsibility for developing provision for people with mental health difficulties has been key to the success of many of the current initiatives reported in this publication. Ideally, there needs to be at least one person appointed to work solely with this group, rather than having a 'portfolio' where they are responsible, for example, for all students with learning difficulties and/or disabilities. Otherwise it can feel like trying to be ambassador for several different countries!

A designated staff member can be crucial in 'holding the threads together' in a situation where different areas of the college or LEA may be involved as well as a number of other agencies. They can also act as powerful advocates for students in ensuring that their learning and support needs are being addressed.

Designated staff can be a powerful catalyst but will only be successful if actively supported by senior managers. This is particularly important if these posts are of relatively low status, and if staff are not necessarily in a position to influence strategic developments. It is a challenge to ensure that provision grows and develops and does not remain marginalised. As this special needs worker commented:

> Staff in discrete 'special needs' type of posts in colleges and LEAs are often working brilliantly and with enormous enthusiasm in terms of their multi-agency role and in their relationships with students. On the other hand they are often marginalised in terms of the whole organisation, get relatively poor support in staff development initiatives and can feel they are always preaching to the converted.

One of the main drawbacks of having a designated worker is that mental health can come to be seen as their sole responsibility is not seen as a whole-organisation responsibility. If the person moves elsewhere or their job changes, the work may lose impetus as this college found:

> Numbers and attendances dwindled last year because the main person took on other responsibilities and their availability and interest and enthusiasm dwindled.

A key role of the specialist worker will be finding ways of embedding the work in the organisation as a whole – moving towards the model of inclusive learning argued for by Tomlinson (FEFC, 1996), endorsed by the FEFC and commended to colleges.

FROM SMALL BEGINNINGS...?

Most current provision grew from modest beginnings; perhaps just two or three classes. This approach has a number of potential advantages.

- If carefully planned and properly delivered, it can demonstrate success at an early stage and be used to make a strong case to senior managers for resourcing more widely. Success tends to breed success.
- It can allow staff to spend the necessary time developing good working alliances within the organisation and with staff in other agencies.
- It can provide opportunities for tutors, learning support staff and staff in health and social services to learn from the experience and use that knowledge to shape future developments.
- By starting on a modest scale, time and attention can be focused on the students and their needs, rather than on organisational issues.

However, it is important to plan for growth and development because small-scale initiatives also have some potential dangers. They:

- may be in danger of being overwhelmed, particularly if the specialist worker becomes seen as the person who will deal with anyone experiencing a mental health crisis;
- can more easily be cut, if savings are needed.

Moving from the margins

> The acceptance in the background of the rest of the college is important. We've been there so long that people are used to us and that makes our job a lot easier. (College lecturer)

Changing individual understandings and practices is not enough if institutional systems and social structures are not themselves changed ... The features of educational systems – entry and progression rules, assessment and evaluation ... financial pressures which limit resources to support different learners – are central to the process of educational marginalisation and exclusion.
(STUART AND THOMSON, 1995: 8)

The 'whole college' approach which promotes inclusive learning will involve a series of measures including improved strategic planning, comprehensive needs analysis, joint planning with health and social services (see Chapter Six), more focused programmes, and raising staff awareness (see Chapter Eleven). Bringing these strands together will, in turn, mean cultivating a strong and committed leadership within the organisation.

If students with mental health difficulties are to be able to move on from discrete provision into mainstream classes, this will necessarily impact on all aspects of the organisation. If they continue only to offer discrete provision, this can easily be marginalised, allowing the college to continue as before without considering the ways in which it may be excluding some learners.

Leadership

Unless senior management is knowledgeable, committed and energetic in the pursuit of creating a good service for students with learning difficulties, the work and dedication of middle management and teachers is diminished or frustrated.
(FEFC, 1996: 8)

Education for adults with mental health difficulties will not enjoy any parity if the staff responsible remain excluded from the power routes and power groups within the college.

Some colleges and LEAs had already found ways of ensuring that senior management are kept informed of their work and support what they are doing. For example:

- Giving presentations to senior managers about the work so that it has a high profile.
- Providing regular written reports to key people in the organisation, so that mental health is on their agendas.
- Presenting information in a positive fashion so that providing for learners with mental health difficulties is not just seen as an act of benevolence and meeting obligations.
- Promoting the work as a positive achievement for the organisation in a competitive and entrepreneurial environment.
- Briefing senior managers about new legislation and national policy developments including relevant developments in mental health.

- Securing political support through meetings, briefings and mailings to local politicians, MPs and MEPs.
- Identifying individuals amongst senior management who may have a particular interest in mental health and who can advocate for this group of learners with their peers.
- Getting publicity for the work in the local media so that the college or LEA is seen to be associated with achievement and success.
- Inviting middle and senior managers to join working groups, etc.
- Holding events to celebrate the students' and the organisation's success and inviting senior staff from education and other services.

As Lancashire County Council found, with their Stepping Stones programme for people with mental health difficulties:

> *Successful innovation requires champions whose role is to support and nurture projects. Often this work [with learners with mental health difficulties] can take place in environments which although not hostile to the innovation can remain indifferent or preoccupied with other priorities.*
> (HOOPER, 1996)

WRITING MENTAL HEALTH INTO POLICIES AND PLANS

Simply producing policies and plans does not necessarily bring about positive change. A college may have a plethora of policy documents but their practice and provision may leave a lot to be desired. On the other hand, one of the most successful schemes identified in this project had no policy documents at all. For plans and policies to be successful they need to be linked to clear implementation strategies with targets for monitoring progress.

Learning opportunities for people with mental health difficulties need to be addressed in:

- Mission statements
- Strategic plans
- Operational plans
- Learning and assessment policies
- Equal opportunities policies
- Disability statements

Raising the profile generally

Strong, committed leadership within the organisation is essential and gives messages to staff and students that mental health is seen as an important issue. Giving mental health a higher profile throughout the organisation can also help to counter any anxieties about people with mental health difficulties joining the student population. Staff training and development (see Chapter Eleven) is one way of tackling this but other initiatives can help too. For example:

- Having specialist staff centrally located so that mental health is seen as literally 'central' – not in a cupboard in a far corner of the building or in a portakabin outside.
- Producing attractive publicity material about specialist provision and making it sure it uses positive language and imagery.

A one-day event at Clarendon College was a huge effort to organise but it generated a great deal of interest in mental health issues both within the college and in the wider community:

> The Mental Health Support Service used World Mental Health Day in 1996 to celebrate their work and as a consciousness-raising event for the whole college. Events were scheduled throughout the day, involving all college areas and all regular teaching was suspended for two hours.
>
> There were fifteen information stalls in the main hall and eighteen workshops were held on Tai Chi, stress-busting and other mental health-related issues. Mental health service users gave a poetry reading and sports students ran events. There was also an art exhibition of works by mental health service users.
>
> The Health Education Authority made a grant available. There was extensive coverage by the local media and the day's events were also videoed for future reference.

PROVISION FOR PARTICULAR GROUPS

Networking with local agencies and forums will often be the best way of identifying unserved or underserved groups. The FEFC's recent publication on needs assessment suggests that:

> colleges should...look to informal and formal networks and liaison groups to identify unexpressed and unmet needs.
>
> (FEFC, 1997C: 70)

Much of the specialist provision described in this publication is targeting 'people with mental health difficulties'. Colleges and LEAs have found that these courses can often meet the needs of individuals with quite diverse requirements. However, some people with mental health difficulties may be unwilling or unable to enrol on these courses and provision which addresses their particular needs may be more appropriate and may offer a positive learning experience.

Our national questionnaire survey and case studies identified provision catering for a range of groups such as:

- women with alcohol problems;
- women from the Bangladeshi community;
- adolescents with school phobias and other mental health difficulties;
- elderly people with dementia;
- African-Caribbean people with mental health difficulties;
- patients in secure units and special hospitals;
- homeless people with mental health difficulties;
- young people with emotional and behavioural difficulties.

The remainder of this section provides a 'snapshot' of the kinds of groups who may benefit from having their own courses, with examples of provision already being made.

WOMEN

Women of all ages are admitted and re-admitted as psychiatric in-patients at a substantially higher rate than men. They are also more likely to be prescribed tranquillizers and anti-depressants (Ashurst and Hall, 1989: 3). Although women can often outnumber men on courses for people with mental health difficulties, women-only provision can cater for women who would not otherwise join a course and can offer a different experience.

In Swindon, for example, the WEA Women's Branch ran two courses in 1996:

> The ten-week courses for women with mental health issues were based around confidence, assertiveness and other personal development issues and were funded by the Laura Ashley Foundation. Women-only groups were essential, enabling participants to raise issues around relationships with men. The 'women-only' setting also meant that women's interests and perspectives were firmly at the centre. The provision of practical support such as childcare was also essential.

In Coventry, the Community Education Service has been working with women with alcohol problems:

> The weekly group is for women who are currently abstaining, controlling or looking for support to achieve their personal goals, and is run by an education worker and a counsellor from the Alcohol Advisory Service. Ten women are currently participating, two others having secured employment and left. The programme was planned with the group and has include craft skills, life skills and alcohol education. Personal development and confidence building have been a focus of the sessions. Although none of the group have yet gained accreditation, all have made progress within all modules (Personal Development, Communication, Planning and Organisation, Groupwork and Craft Skills).

MINORITY ETHNIC COMMUNITIES

As NIACE pointed out in its evidence to the Tomlinson Committee:

> *ethnic minority communities [are] under-represented in provision and little atten-*
> *tion has been paid as yet to issues of race and disability in curriculum or staff*
> *development.*
>
> (NIACE, 1994: PARA 28)

Our national survey of colleges and LEAs confirmed this. Very few respondents were making any specialist provision in this area. Education provision is often neither ethno-centric nor ethno-sensitive.

There is also considerable evidence suggesting that mental health services are failing to provide appropriately for black and other minority ethnic communities (Jennings, 1996). However, some agencies are striving to develop better services and the Government is committed to improving local authority provision for people from minority ethnic communities with severe mental illness, through the Mental Illness Specific Grant (DoH, 1997: 12).

The needs of people with mental health difficulties from minority ethnic communities are extremely diverse and education providers will need to work closely with other community-based organisations.

In Lambeth, the Community Education Service has been working with Black mental health service users for over ten years:

> The Fanon Trust (formerly Brixton Circle) offers support and advice, counselling, education and social activities for black people with mental health difficulties. The Trust has a day centre, a hostel, a training scheme and a women's project. Lambeth CES has been providing tutor hours for the last ten years, working with clients and managers to plan and deliver a curriculum which has included basic education, creative writing, drama, health education, arts and crafts, music and photography. The centre's manager is involved in interviewing new tutors to help ensure the recruitment of tutors who understand the effects of economic and social deprivation and racism. A unified approach which aims to empower students is central to this partnership.

Developing provision which takes account of cultural beliefs and practices is essential as Nelson and Colne College discovered:

> The College has an Asian women's support group which is run jointly by a counsellor and a bilingual support worker. Play facilities are available for children so that women can attend. Although many of the women who attend are are emotionally vulnerable, terms such as 'mental illness' are avoided as they are not culturally acceptable. Recruitment has been through visiting the women in their own homes. Women are bringing other women along and attendance is increasing steadily.

ELDERLY PEOPLE WITH DEMENTIA

The most common mental health problems in old age are anxiety and sleep disorders, but six per cent of people over 65 suffer from dementia (DoH, 1996), characterised by memory loss and confusion. Although dementia is usually progressive, a strong case has been made for maintaining the individual's 'personhood' through empathic communication which can counter withdrawal and increasing dependency (Goldsmith, 1996).

Education can offer opportunities for communication both individually and within groups as the following examples of provision for elderly people with dementias illustrate.

> York WEA has been running reminiscence groups for elderly confused women, with funding from Social Services. By keeping memories alive, their sense of personal identity is reinforced, and short- and long-term memories are stimulated. Sharing memories with others increases social skills and self-confidence and people have the chance to develop listening as well as verbal skills.
>
> Lambeth Community Education Service has been running creative communication classes at a day centre for people with dementia who would otherwise be unable to access community education provision. This two-hour class was developed by social workers, managers and the CES tutor, though actual sessions are student-led, rather than using a more curriculum-based approach. Through craft, art, drama, music and discussion, these older students are experiencing many benefits. They are more positive, better able to make choices, more confident and more able to socialise with other people around them.

YOUNG PEOPLE

Increasing attention is now being paid to the mental health of young people. Between the ages of 13 and 19, up to one in five young people will require help for problems such as eating disorders, self-harm, alcohol or drug abuse, or behaviours worrying to them and their families (DoH, 1996b)

Through liaison with schools and other services for children and young people, colleges and LEAs can offer support for vulnerable young people to make the transition from school to further education. This is already happening in York:

> A Learning Support Tutor from York College has been attending meetings at the Adolescent Unit run by the Mental Health NHS Trust to facilitate transition planning for young people coming up to college age. The College also plans to develop pre-entry work with other local agencies such as the Pupil Support Service, the Careers Service, school pastoral staff and educational social workers. The College also has nine students on full-time mainstream courses who are supported through a joint LEA- and TEC-funded initiative for 14-16 year old non-attenders (although this group do not necessarily have identified mental health difficulties).
>
> West Nottingham College has recently established a partnership with an LEA unit for school students who have been excluded and from September 1997 six students will be spending two days a week on the college campus.

HOMELESS PEOPLE

Although not all homeless people have mental health difficulties, the closure of long-stay hospitals, coupled with shorter in-patient stays for acute episodes, has swelled the numbers of homeless men and women with a history of mental ill-health.

Although financing education provision for homeless people can be difficult, the York Branch of the WEA has found it to be a worthwhile and rewarding area of work, despite the difficulties. As the Organiser, Helen Widdowson, reports:

> At Peaseholme Centre [for homeless people], the WEA has been running Arts and Crafts sessions. Students' work has been on display at the Centre, increasing numbers are attending and everyone is pleased with the way things are going. The Life Skills Course has also been very successful, even though numbers attending have sometimes been very small. Staff have commented on the personal development of those taking part. The main problem is that students are unlikely to remain constant throughout the course due to the high turnover of clients using the Centre so it is difficult to know how to pitch the course.

MENTALLY DISORDERED OFFENDERS

The Reed Committee (DoH, 1992), which reviewed services to mentally disordered offenders, recommended the provision of adult and further education in all secure units. However, provision remains patchy and there are wide variations in the number of hours tuition made available.

The educational needs of mentally disordered offenders will be as diverse as with any group of adult learners but providers working in secure units have drawn attention to the following issues:

- there is currently no coherent national strategy for provision;
- teaching staff in secure units can often be very isolated;
- provision has to accommodate students who will be in secure units for many years, and others who will only be there for a brief period;
- an education programme has to cater for people with university degrees as well as people who may have substantial learning difficulties.

Despite these challenges, education can make a very positive contribution to the lives of mentally disordered offenders. It can enhance the quality of life while they remain in secure facilities but can also be a 'bridge' into the outside world when someone is discharged into the community. The long-term future of special hospitals is now in doubt and there is growing support for a network of smaller, dispersed NHS units where people can be treated nearer their families. If these changes are implemented, the demand for education in secure provision is likely to increase.

Needs analysis

As noted above, existing education provision targeting adults with mental health difficulties has developed from many different starting-points, often as the result of someone seeing a 'window of opportunity'. If education providers are to reach currently under-represented groups and be responsive to the community as a whole, they will need to identify the scope and nature of unmet needs.

To assist in this task, the FEFC commissioned the Institute for Employment Studies to produce a practical guide for colleges (FEFC, 1997b). The Guide gives useful advice and suggests complementary approaches including closer liaison with other agencies – the theme of the next chapter.

■ KEY THEMES AND ISSUES

- Less than half of all colleges and Local Education Authorities surveyed had a designated person responsible for adults with mental health difficulties.

- The catalysts for developing provision were many and varied in the organisations surveyed. Sometimes developments rested on a key person's enthusiasm, which can lead to fragility unless provision is embedded.

- The support of senior managers is crucial. A range of strategies has been used to canvass support from senior staff, to include briefings and celebratory events.

- Some courses are targeted at particular groups of people with mental health difficulties such as:
  - ■ women
  - ■ alcoholics
  - ■ homeless people
  - ■ young adults
  - ■ elderly people with dementia
  - ■ mentally disordered offenders

- The survey showed that very few areas are offering provision targeted at people with mental health difficulties from black and ethnic minorities.

■ QUESTIONS

- Does your college/Local Education Authority have a post with designated responsibility for continuing education for adults with mental health difficulties?

- Do existing or planned developments have the support of senior managers?

- Can briefings/training be arranged for senior staff on the key issues?

- What needs analysis has been done/needs to be done to ensure that marginalised groups of adults with mental health difficulties can access learning?

- What targeted provision exists/could be developed for groups of adults with mental health difficulties such as women, homeless people, young adults, older adults and people from black and other minority ethnic groups?

CHAPTER SIX

BUILDING ALLIANCES

*...only through effective partnership and collaboration can agencies reach more
and different adult learners...The Government recognises that no single agency
can by itself transform the UK into a learning society.*
(TUCKETT, 1997: 9, 10)

The development of strong alliances between education providers and other
organisations involved with people with mental health difficulties is crucial.
As Alan Tuckett says, partnership working is essential if people who currently
have difficulty gaining access to educational opportunities are to become part of
an inclusive learning society. Peter Bates echoes this, reminding us that partnership is not just about bringing agencies and professionals together: collaboration
means gathering together the different strands which go to make up a person's
life and developing support which is consistent and coherent across all the
strands.

Inter-agency working is essential since no single organisation or agency can
provide for all the aspects required.

*...the community is arbitrarily broken up into manageable 'life domains' such as
employment, further education, voluntary work, arts, sports and neighbourhood
associations...A champion is found for each life domain, who will build partnerships with the other agencies working in this area, and invent ways of supporting
users to access those opportunities.*
(BATES, 1996: 28)

Inter-agency working does not happen of its own accord. Successful collaboration
requires commitment from all parties to develop multi-agency approaches and a
willingness to match words with action. Partnership was central to the best of the

provision we encountered during this project. Others had identified this as a weakness in their work. Respondents to the national survey identified some of the gaps:

> Not enough liaison at strategic level. (LEA)
>
> We lack input from the voluntary sector. (LEA)
>
> We need a more coherent approach by all professionals involved in providing support. (LEA)
>
> [Unmet needs include] inter-agency networking. (FE college)

THE BENEFITS OF COLLABORATION

For education providers, working together with other agencies has numerous benefits including:

- pooling of skills and resources (including finance);
- providing opportunities for mutual learning, both informally and through structured training opportunities;
- ensuring greater understanding of the contribution of other services to the lives of people with mental health difficulties and greater likelihood of developing complementary services;
- providing help with identifying students' learning support needs and how these can best be met;
- developing a wider choice of day-time and evening activities;
- generating networks in the community for circulating information about educational opportunities;
- developing provision based on the identified needs and wishes of mental health service users;
- providing a more holistic approach to meeting the needs of individuals.
- offering access to different and complementary perspectives and to a wider range of contacts in the community.

Challenges to developing successful alliances

Working with other agencies can be challenging, uncomfortable and frustrating. Progress can be impeded when:

- there is a lack of commitment to partnership at a senior level;
- organisations have no shared vision, principles and goals;
- there is a failure to understand each other's roles and responsibilities;
- there seem to be no tangible goals or clear outcomes;
- partner organisations fail to understand each other's history, culture, professional ethos and working practices;
- there is a lack of trust and openness between partners.

On the other hand, alliances are more likely to succeed if:

- there is a shared vision;
- an agreed agenda for joint action has been established;
- each partner is doing whatever they have agreed to do;
- there are identified mechanisms for collaboration;
- priorities have been agreed;
- there is mutual respect and trust
- participants are willing to learn from one another;
- people are sensitive to other agencies' cultures and working practices and aware of their concerns;
- communication between organisations occurs at each level.

A shared vision

> *Vision: a highly imaginative scheme (OED) a picture formed in the mind*
> (LAROUSSE)

Partnership works best when the players have a shared picture of what it is they are working towards – in this case, what a better lifestyle for people with mental health difficulties would look like. As the government emphasised in *Health of the Nation*: 'What drives alliance building is the conviction that working together gives better opportunities for improving health…' (DoH, 1997: 23).

Collaborative working arrangements are set up for all sorts of reasons. For example:

- College managers may approach an NHS Trust because they are aware that people with mental health difficulties are an untapped market.
- A residential service provider may approach the local adult education service because residents have no regular daytime activities and registration officers have asked them to address this need.

Whatever brings two organisations together, it is worth spending some time clarifying what the desired outcomes will be for service users. Placing users/learners at the centre, whether through a shared mission statement or agreed aims or, ideally, by involving them directly, can help keep everyone focused on the reasons they got together in the first place.

A common agenda

If provision is to develop in a planned and structured way and is to reach more potential learners, education needs to get onto mental health agendas, including community care plans, so that it is seen as a distinctive part of a range of provision of daytime and evening activities.

Our national survey asked colleges and LEAs if:

- they were involved in inter-agency planning for people with mental health difficulties;
- local authority community care plans made any specific reference to adult education for people with mental health difficulties.

The results showed that there is still a long way to go, particularly in the case of community care plans. Education for people with mental health difficulties was mentioned in less than a quarter (23.6 per cent) of plans.

On the other hand, over a third (37.6 per cent) of college and LEA staff were involved with formal and informal planning activities with a wide range of organisations. For example:

- locality planning group for mental health;
- local mental health advisory group;

- TEC working group on mental health;
- inter-agency planning group (health, social services, LEA and voluntary organisations);
- planning group for day centre development;
- mental health locality advisory group;
- executive committee of local association of drop-ins;
- joint care planning team;
- joint probation/mental health team;
- care development planning team (social services);
- working party on growth and development of user-led services;
- mental health day care forum.

FINDING YOUR ALLIES

Opportunities for collaboration may present themselves: a college may be asked to run some courses in a hospital, for example, or a day centre may request input from the adult education service. But education providers need to work with a much wider range of agencies and groups than the main mental health service providers – not least because by no means everyone with mental health difficulties is a mental health service user.

Organisations involved with vocational training or supported employment may be useful allies if education providers need contacts who can help people find work. The local volunteer bureau may be able to find befrienders to support students on mainstream courses. Thinking about our own networks of friends and contacts may also be helpful. It's surprising how useful friends (or friends of friends!) can be.

Sometimes the most useful allies are the people or organisations that may not seem particularly obvious – but may be on the doorstep. Some education providers have made good links with their local authority – with a women's unit, or an economic development unit, or equal opportunities team. Working with people outside the mental health system can be particularly useful because they offer different perspectives – and will have their own networks of contacts to tap into.

Alliances – not merger?

Education providers need to work closely with other agencies, but also need to maintain a separate and distinctive identity. This is particularly important for students who also use mental health services. Although collaboration between education staff and mental health professionals is often necessary and beneficial (see Chapter Eight), students benefit from moving into a different environment, leaving behind the role of 'patient' or 'client'. Specialist educational provision and support must not be seen as another – or even alternative – mental health service, but as a complementary one with a distinctive role to play.

Resourcing alliance-building

Involvement with other agencies can be time-consuming as this college lecturer commented:

> I'd like to go to the Mental Health Day Care Forum once a month, I'd like to go to the Joint Community Care Planning Group that meets three times a term…and that is without all the internal meetings that we have.

Regular communication including opportunities for meeting colleagues from other agencies are essential if education is to feature on health and social services agendas. It needs to be on strategic planning agendas, operational plans and an option for all individual care plans. As the lecturer quoted above added:

> I am constantly saying at the Day Care Forum, 'education, education' It must be part of people's plans and part of strategic plans.

Specialist staff in adult and further education are working under increasing pressure and there is some evidence that time allocated to liaison with other agencies and non-student contact is being cut back. This is a false economy. Without a sound network of contacts with mental health agencies and community organisations, education staff will not have the necessary referral networks, and will find it hard to access the knowledge and skills of mental health professionals. Spending time developing alliances will also help establish the credibility of educational provision with mental health service providers and users.

Justifying the costs of attending meetings in other organisations can be difficult when there may appear to be no direct benefits. If education is to become part of health and social services agendas, then education providers must be there since agendas are generally shaped by those who are actually sitting round the table.

Collaboration at all levels

Alliances can be formed to undertake planning at a strategic level or provide support to an individual student. These should not be seen as alternatives. Collaboration needs to develop at all levels in organisations from senior managers through to learning support staff.

Collaboration often appears to work well at an operational level but progress can be hampered by a lack of commitment to joint working at higher levels. Staff in one LEA found:

> Local education authority staff felt that strong alliances had been developed with mental health services staff at an operational level. As a result, a charge nurse and senior occupational therapist had approached the health authority requesting funding to develop adult education provision. The request was refused. LEA staff felt this was because there was a lack of understanding and communication at a level which could affect policy and funding decisions.

A range of collaborative approaches

Collaboration often starts with individuals from different agencies meeting and deciding they can work together. That can often be extremely effective, but the problem with collaboration built on personal contacts is that people leave, change jobs and move on. Unless there are more formal mechanisms, partnerships can be difficult to sustain. Having specific structures for joint working also gives clear messages to staff that collaboration is accepted as an essential feature of provision.

The following examples demonstrate clearly how collaborative approaches can be successful in achieving specified outcomes and in providing a more coherent, effective service.

BUILDING MULTIPLE ALLIANCES

REMIT is a mental health project based at a community college in Leicester. It grew out of an initial alliance between the LEA's Basic Skills provision and the Special Needs service, working together with the health authority and social services. REMIT has subsequently developed further alliances with the City Council, the incorporated colleges, primary health care teams, voluntary organisations, user groups and private providers.

CO-TUTORING A COURSE

In the East Riding of Yorkshire, a MIND worker and a Community Education tutor have co-tutored a course on managing panic attacks. After piloting the course in one venue, a training pack was developed and the course is currently being run in a second location. Links with MIND resulted in ten self-referrals to the second course after it was publicised in the MIND Newsletter. This has also been a 'learning together' exercise since the course has been attended by mental health workers as well as service users.

A JOINTLY FUNDED RESEARCH PROJECT

Southwark Day Care Forum in South London which represents providers and users of community care day services commissioned a study which asked people with mental health difficulties what they wanted from education services. The study was funded by Southwark Social Services, using Mental Illness Specific Grant monies, with matched funds from Southwark Adult Education Institute (now part of Southwark College).

NETWORKING IN EDUCATION, TRAINING AND REHABILITATION

Lewisham's Community Education Service belongs to Network whose other members include five mental health projects and four mainstream training agencies. Network brings together work training and rehabilitation agencies, to work collaboratively, avoid duplication, integrate people with mental health problems into mainstream services and encourage user participation.

SHARED STAFF TRAINING AND DEVELOPMENT

The Norfolk Adult Education Service worked for 18 months with patients at Hellesdon Hospital. One of the project's aims was that nursing staff would be able to explore the way they perceived the residents and how they worked with them. Seven hospital staff did the City and Guilds Stage I Tutor Training Course as part of their professional development, alongside seven adult education tutors. Nursing staff became much more aware of the learning potential of people with mental health difficulties as well as having the chance to acquire new skills, and two nurses went on to do Stage II of the C&G course to qualify as FE teachers.

COLLABORATION INVOLVING PRIMARY CARE

The Handling Stress Course on Prescription in Humberside is a multi- agency initiative – a 'healthy alliance', as their leaflet describes it, between a local GP practice, the Adult Education Service, the Pavilion Leisure Centre and Hull and Holderness Community Health NHS Trust. The GPs are able to prescribe a seven-week course on handling stress to help people recognise stressful situations and develop ways of coping with them. Two-hourly sessions are held every week at the Leisure Centre and the course is free.

INTER-AGENCY SUPERVISION

The Mental Health Support Service at Clarendon College was established as a joint initiative by local education and mental health services. When the Education Counsellor was appointed to run the service, she had monthly supervision sessions with a mental health professional to talk about any aspects of her work. The aim of this cross-over was to help the Education Counsellor key her work into positive mental health practice. The Support Service has always sought to ensure that the Education Counsellor's interventions with students complement those of mental health services staff. It has never been the intention to create a new breed of mental health professional working in education.

Learning about each other

> *Education has a great deal to offer people with mental health problems, but access to the service very often depends on health...or community staff. It is vital that they appreciate what education has to offer.*
> (MAIN, 1996: 3)

Building alliances with other agencies gives staff the chance to learn how other organisations operate and what they can offer people with mental health difficulties. Mental health professionals may have a very limited understanding of the role of education for adults. For example, they may believe that:

- it is only about vocational training;
- people can only enrol if they are completely well;
- it offers much the same as the occupational therapy service;
- people can only start a course in September;
- education for adults is really just like they remember school.

Not everyone would agree with the psychiatrist who said that in his hospital 'we are all teachers!' but indirectly it does point to the fact that roles can be blurred. An adult education class can often be therapeutic and occupational therapists and nurses can find themselves teaching people. Teachers can find this confusing; as this adult education tutor reflected:

> I've done quite a lot of thinking on how I see my role as a tutor. It can be quite confusing at times. It's important to relate to people but I'm not a counsellor or a therapist. I relate to people as people, like in a mainstream class and I try to be focused on the issues around the photography and not get into things outside that role.

The fact that different professionals are involved in similar activities means that there is a need for each agency to be clear about its own role and how that relates to the work of other agencies. Education providers need to communicate clearly to other agencies that:

- education has something positive to offer people with mental health difficulties;

- people with mental health difficulties do have the potential to learn and can benefit from access to learning opportunities;
- participation in education can be a bridge to new opportunities;
- discrete provision is not 'day care in a college building';
- education is not a mental health service but can complement and support the work of mental health services.

Education providers and mental health agencies have to find out about each other. They need to learn from one another. Mental health services need to understand what education can offer and education needs to ask what people might want to learn, how they might learn and what kind of approaches are likely to work best. Each needs the other and can benefit from the partnership. As this college lecturer commented:

> What is important is recognising who we are – that we are teachers first. And one of the things we are going to be looking at is support mechanisms, what they should be, how we should contact people in emergencies and so on.

Reaching an understanding of what another organisation can offer may take time, though it can eventually be beneficial as this college found:

> Social Services now fund 40 places [on two college courses] but this only happened after quite a struggle. It was a real problem getting recognition and support to begin with, but now they can see the benefits to people.

Encouraging people to enrol at college should not be seen as a strategy for closing the day centre or freeing up places for new people, unless current users have indicated they want alternatives to current services. As one lecturer warned, 'I think there's a danger of being seen as a dumping ground.' Embarking on an education programme should be a positive choice, not a mechanism for moving people round between services.

Learning about other agencies also involves each partner thinking about boundaries, being clear about what the college or adult education provider does and what needs to be provided by other agencies, for example, in relation to learning support (see Chapter Nine).

KEY THEMES AND ISSUES

- Partnership and collaboration are vital to build a coherent, effective service.

- The project survey respondents identified gaps in liaison and inter-agency working.

- A shared vision, a common agenda and a network of allies all contribute to an effective partnership.

- Example of collaboration are diverse, and range from shared funding to GPs prescribing stress management courses.

- Learning about each agency's distinct role/remit helps towards a shared understanding.

QUESTIONS

- Who are the key partners and allies in your area – or who could be? Make a list and think as widely as possible.

- What strengths and what gaps are there in relation to liaison and inter-agency working in your area?

- Do agencies share a common vision or agenda, or are there different view points? How central is education to the agenda?

- What examples of collaboration are there in your area?

- Is there scope for shared training, to help different agencies understand each other's way of working?

CHAPTER SEVEN

FUNDING

Securing the necessary funding to develop and maintain provision is a great concern for managers and practitioners alike. This chapter does not offer any magic wands, but outlines approaches which have been used, many of which rely on a partnership approach. It also looks at some of the difficulties in relation to funding. Lastly, it considers the position of learners themselves: students with mental health difficulties may be on very low incomes, so it is quite possible that the cost of any course fees, materials and travel expenses costs may be a financial worry for them.

The Further and Higher Education Act (1992)

The Further and Higher Education Act (1992) changed the way in which continuing education was funded when it was implemented in 1993. It split responsibilities for funding and ensuring adequate provision between local education authorities and the Further Education Funding Councils in England and Wales. The local education authorities were given responsibility for non-vocational education. The FEFC was given responsibility for funding vocational, academic and basic education, as well as associated preparatory courses which are defined in Schedule 2 of the Act. The funding methodology devised by FEFC has been welcomed in many respects and has offered some new possibilities, such as the opportunity to fund support for individuals through the learning support bands.

However, some issues are unresolved. Information gathered during the Tomlinson Committee's work highlighted some of the particular difficulties in matching current FEFC funding to the needs of learners with mental health difficulties. The FEDA/NIACE project survey and case studies identified examples of specific problems, which are outlined later in this chapter.

Sources of funding

The project survey asked colleges and LEAs to identify sources of funding for students with mental health difficulties. Survey responses indicated that 37 per cent of FE college provision for people with mental health difficulties was funded by the FEFC, a further 12 per cent by LEAs and 6 per cent through joint finance. In contrast, adult education responses indicated that 21 per cent of provision for people with mental health difficulties was funded by the LEA, with 8.5 per cent funded by the health authority. Of the remaining LEA provision, 6 per cent was supported by joint finance and 6 per cent was funded by FEFC. Other funding sources were also mentioned and are included in the list of funders below. This list is not definitive, but includes the range of funders mentioned in the project survey, with specific examples where these have been available.

Funding source	Examples of expenditure (where available)
Further Education Funding Council	• accredited vocational and academic programmes • basic education programmes • additional learning support such as additional advice and guidance, counselling and assessment • transport required by the college course • quality initiative to develop inclusive learning in 1997/8 via staff development
Local Education Authorities	• non-vocational education • transport from home to training institution • schedule 2 provision via FEFC

Training and Enterprise Councils	• training programmes, travel costs
European Social Fund	• training, guidance, beneficiary costs such as travel, childcare (not full costs)
Mental Illness Specific Grant (MISG)	• mental health advocacy training
Fundholding GPs	• advice, counselling
City Challenge	• training programmes, travel costs, additional support costs
Joint Finance	• contribution to projects/staffing costs
Social Services Departments	• care in the community projects
NHS Mental Health Trusts	• support for hospital classes and transition
District Health Authorities	
Other local authority departments (e.g. Youth Service)	
Students' fees	• can contribute to covering costs
Voluntary organisations	• MIND involvement via local groups in education initiatives
Charitable trusts	• local, regional or national grants
Regional arts bodies	• funding for arts projects

The following examples indicate how funding from a range of sources has been used in practice:

> The Survivors' Network in Haringey, facilitated by a service user, is funded by the LEA and MIND jointly.

Bolton Community Education Service has MISG funding for mental health advocacy training.

A GP fundholder paid for one-to-one guidance as part of a package of support for a patient with mental health difficulties.

Leicester City Council's special needs training funded paid for the development of a non-health-based assessment and for REMIT staff to visit other projects.

In Leicestershire, social services allocate a sum of money which is redistributed to different County Council departments for any work which implements care in the community, which includes community education, transport, etc.

The Speedwell Project in Lewisham has a grant from Deptford Health Challenge Connections initiative which funds research and supports a group for former project users who have moved into education or training courses or employment.

These examples clearly demonstrate that funding can be obtained from a range of sources to support educational opportunities. The only limitation appears to be the imagination and time to explore funding opportunities with other partners. However, education staff have expressed concerns that they are spending too much time chasing funds.

A collaborative approach

People with mental health difficulties seeking education and training will have a range of needs, abilities and achievements as learners. People may well need services from a wide range of agencies, including support from health and social services, the benefits agency, housing organisations and day care services, as well as education and training providers. It can be complex to put a relevant package together. Each of these agencies will be funded differently and will have various funding frameworks to draw upon, each with its own target groups, services and constraints. An individual with mental health difficulties may need to draw upon a range of agencies and no single service is likely to be able to meet all the needs of any one individual. A multi-agency approach is essential, with funding and provision drawn from a variety of sources. A 'mixed' funding package should be regularly reviewed as the person's needs change.

As a result, learning and support will be funded and delivered through a range of services. It is common to find funding packages for particular programmes where different elements, such as tutor costs, classroom support and transport, are financed from different sources. Inevitably, the detailed package of funding will vary according to individuals' needs, the organisation(s) which they attend and their learning goals. One example would be a programme for people being resettled from long-stay hospitals or for former day centre users. It may have transition provision at a local FE college funded as part of a social services- or health-supported programme, with basic skills (or accredited vocational training and learning support elements) funded by the FEFC. A similar programme at an adult education institute, where the learner is undertaking a programme of leisure or craft-based study which is not accredited, may be funded through local education authority and social services budgets.

This type of funding package is most likely to be found in provision targeted at the point of transition from a health or social services organisation into education or training. It is likely that funding will be drawn from a variety of sources and that provision to meet support needs may change as the situation develops, as the following example illustrates:

> The Finding a Future course at the College of NE London was originally set up with funding from health and social services. The learning programmes subsequently developed were eligible for funding under Schedule 2, so that the FEFC now funds this provision, with the health service paying for a link worker.

Towards a funding strategy

In order to ensure that educational opportunities for people with mental health difficulties are developed in a way which is responsive to individual learning requirements, the following principles need to be considered:

- recognition that students often need extended pre-entry advice and guidance, as well as ongoing support;

- resourcing and time for specialist staff to make links and liaise with staff from other organisations to build effective collaborative working relationships;
- flexibility to accommodate periods of interrupted learning where necessary, through a modular framework;
- recognition that some students will require extra time in order to achieve accreditation, while for others getting a certificate may not be on their personal agenda;
- stability and continuity to minimise uncertainty and anxiety amongst students;
- partnership with other providers in the community to ensure the best use of resources;
- external funding which meets the needs of service users, so that provision is needs-led rather than funding-led.

WHAT ARE THE BARRIERS IN RELATION TO FUNDING?

Short-term funding

Project or development funding is often short-term, which can lead to uncertainty for both staff and students. One project with an excellent record has been struggling to survive at the time of going to press. The sense is that much of the provision is still very fragile.

Planning cycles

The planning cycles of different agencies involved in a multi-agency approach often vary, which can cause difficulties in the continuity of provision and funding. Each bid is also likely to have to compete against other priorities. Involvement in joint planning also takes time. One senior practitioner used to be allocated time to attend joint planning meetings, but this has been stopped as a "luxury" by the college which has taken over the provision. Longer term this may prove to have been a short-sighted move, as it will make it harder for education to be on the agenda of health and social services and hence less likely to be funded.

Accreditation

In order to be eligible for FEFC funding, programmes need to be externally accredited or to demonstrate progression towards accredited courses. This is misinterpreted by some organisations, who wrongly assume that all provision needs to be accredited and consequently limit their curriculum range to accredited programmes.

The focus on accreditation and individual listing of qualifications has led to more provision becoming accredited. This can mean that some programmes are designed to meet accreditation outcomes rather than to fulfil the learning needs of people with mental health difficulties.

Irregular attendance

Tracking systems which provide evidence for funding claims do not easily allow for intermittent attendance patterns. For example, a learner with mental health difficulties can have recurrent episodes of ill health, which cause him or her to drop in and out of study. To a large extent, the existing systems assume that individuals will attend regularly and that they will be enrolled and attending at prescribed census dates during each term. An organisation may see it as being in its own interests to enrol only learners who are likely to be consistent in their attendance. This approach causes potential difficulties for students whose attendance is erratic due to ill health.

Pressure to succeed

Many qualifications are listed within the FEFC's methodology and the level of funding for them is based upon the average number of hours that have been used for delivery, within the further education sector. As a result, pressure may be exerted to encourage learners to complete programmes and achieve full accreditation within a specific time period. This is unhelpful to those with mental ill health, for whom patterns of completion and achievement are likely to be erratic and uneven. This will be compounded where learners are enrolled but find regular attendance difficult. A staff member in a case study commented that:

> So far, students experiencing an episode of mental ill-health have managed to struggle through and complete their assignments on time and get to the end of the course but...

She expressed concerns that the time pressure had created difficulties and it was unlikely that all students would continue to succeed.

Variable rates of funding

Funding levels will vary according to the funding source. There are no shared indicators of value for money or agreed levels of funding for a particular activity. Training programmes which attract European Social Funding through Objective 3 or INTEGRA, for example, may allow more generous levels of funding per student hour, and also offer funding for a range of eligible beneficiary costs. TEC-funded programmes may attract additional funding for learners identified as having 'Special Training Needs,' but will require that eligibility is assessed, often by non-specialist advisers.

Programmes in the voluntary sector may have a much lower level of resource, with some supported by fund-raising activities and small scale grants. They may attract additional unpaid support through volunteers, peppercorn rents, etc. Even within individual funding streams there will be variations: for example, in relation to FEFC funding, the level of funding for different organisations can vary. LEA adult education provision varies dramatically across England and Wales, while some services have been the victims of savage cuts in recent years. The debate about 'adequacy' and what it means in relation to LEA adult education provision is a matter of hot debate. The forthcoming White Paper on Lifelong Learning in late 1997 is eagerly awaited.

The disparity in levels of funding were summed up by one county special needs worker, who commented: 'It remains an uneven playing field'.

FUNDING TENSIONS

Each funding source will have competing demands made upon it. In the education sector, the FEDA/NIACE survey uncovered some of the following tensions:

- Many FE institutions are experiencing reducing levels of overall FEFC funding and may have reduced opportunities to develop new areas of provision and to grow. Learners with mental health difficulties may be able to attract additional units for entry guidance and on programme support, but some colleges will experience a tension between choosing to provide appropriate provision for a relatively small number of learners (each attracting a higher level of funding) or widening participation to a larger number of learners who may have lower levels of learning support needs;

- The pace and pressure of the move to cut down on unit costs in the education sector means that many colleges plan to reduce delivery hours for courses, increase class sizes and improve student retention. All of these factors may act to the disadvantage of learners with mental health difficulties;

- In their strategic planning, FE colleges are required to carry out a needs analysis and to indicate how they intend to address any unmet needs. In many areas, a number of education and training organisations may be competing for the same learner groups. People with mental health difficulties may be seen as new customers, but they may be also be seen as a financial risk because of their patterns of attendance and achievements;

- People with mental health difficulties may be eligible for concessionary fees or may be charged no fee. However, the study revealed an example of clearly discriminatory practice. In one case, learners with mental health difficulties were offered classes at reduced fee rates, but were only given places if there were spaces left after full-fee-paying students had enrolled;

- Where funding sources have very precise limitations on support for additional learning needs (such as Higher Education and some TEC funded programmes), the learner with complex and significant support needs is likely to be disadvantaged. Writing about the impact of market values on Higher Education, Halton suggests:

The constant search for finance adversely affects what can be provided for students. While the enrolling student is a source of income, the enrolled student with needs is an unwelcome cost.

(HALTON, 1995: 193)

- Although joint finance can be a useful source, it tends to be time-limited and development-orientated. It has been instrumental in enabling new provision to develop. However, grants are usually tapered and cannot always be replaced with new or equal amounts of funding from elsewhere.

> Adult education work in a medium secure unit was 100 per cent joint-financed for two years. Despite lobbying by staff, the funding was not extended. A smaller grant was provided through the rehabilitation fund and the mental health trust, but this only covers direct teaching costs. Consequently, education staff are no longer able to be a part of the multi-disciplinary assessment team.

- In all educational provision, classes are liable to close if recruitment targets are not reached or if attendance numbers fall too low. This is disappointing for any student, but for people with mental health difficulties for whom the effort of joining may have been a major challenge, it can present a major setback.

Competition for resources occurs in health and social services too. Although both are significant contributors to the cost of current provision, mental health services in many areas are under huge pressure to fund acute and long-term care. Education will find it is competing with other services providers for the same pot of money.

> The future of our work looks very bleak as the Trust's Elderly Mental Health Services are seriously overspent and they have been told they have to cut a further large amount next year. As a result they have decided to cut all 'extras', including the reminiscence sessions.
>
> Health may be reluctant to pay (for adult education) – it's a choice between an auxiliary who'll be there all week or a tutor for two sessions.

Programme continuity

As a student with mental health difficulties progresses from one type of provision to another, the changes in funding may mean that a particular type of support is no longer available or very difficult to secure. Continuity between programmes can be lost at the precise moment when the learner is most vulnerable to change.

- Funding arrangements enabling people to access education while in health service accommodation may be discontinued when someone moves into the community. For example, offenders are entitled to receive education while in health service secure accommodation, but this often stops at the point when they leave – when education could be an important 'bridge' into the community.

> One tutor was approached to put on a yoga class in the community for people with mental health difficulties leaving the hospital, but funding could not be secured.

The availability of consistent support is an important factor in ensuring that the learning environment adequately matches the learner's needs. It may become tapered or tail off as the learner progresses within education and training, but a sharp cut off when a learner transfers to a new programme is not generally appropriate.

Issues of student finance

The project identified several factors which need to be considered in terms of financial support for learners with mental health difficulties. It supports the view expressed in the FEFC's chief inspector's report and *Learning Works* that financial support is a major issue for students.

- the majority of learners with mental health difficulties will be receiving benefits and/or be on low incomes, so any costs for fees, materials or examinations need to be kept as low as possible;
- students are often very anxious about whether entering education will affect their benefits. There is a also a high level of anxiety about the security of benefits and the effect apparent 'recovery' may have;
- anxiety about personal finance can get in the way of learning and even lead to drop-out and failure;
- issues related to finance need to be addressed at the pre-entry guidance

stage and referral to welfare advisers may be necessary. Help can be given with applications to trusts or charities;

- students in FE do not have an entitlement to a grant and the availability of discretionary awards varies from one LEA to another and is also very limited;
- students on full-time higher education courses may be eligible for the disabled students' allowance. This grant is due to be revamped with the end of free tuition for all students. Some students with mental health difficulties may not be well enough to study full-time so may not receive financial assistance.

One way in which organisations can assist students is through a policy of concessionary fees.

A NEW TOMORROW?

The FEFC report *Learning Works* recommends widening participation and adapting funding patterns to support students who are currently missing out. If these recommendations are implemented, they should hopefully be wide enough to include and benefit potential learners with mental health difficulties. In parallel, the FEFC has set up an implementation committee to try and ensure that key recommendations from the *Inclusive Learning* report will actually happen. Some recommendations relate directly to funding and students with mental health difficulties, such as the suggestion that start-up funding is required to establish new provision for under-represented groups.

At the time of writing (October 1997), the Department for Education and Employment is considering how best to spend the £195 million pounds from the windfall tax, which has been pledged by government to enable unemployed disabled people to gain employment. This funding is in addition to the money which will be spent on the Welfare to Work initiative, which includes the New Deal programmes. The £195 million will expand employment opportunities for unemployed people on disability benefits, to include invalidity benefit and incapacity benefit. The funding will be spent over the next four years and is as yet unallocated. The money could be perhaps used to demonstrate what works and what the gaps are, in order to inform future planning. Consideration of regional variations would also be important. The measure is also reinforced by the setting up of a social exclusion task force at 10 Downing Street.

Lastly, the Government has shown a clear commitment to adult learning in setting up the National Advisory Group on Continuing Education and Lifelong Learning (NAGCELL) and to producing a forthcoming White Paper on this topic, due out late autumn 1997. The theme of moving from exclusion towards inclusion and participation for all learners is a topic central to the committee's core work, while the draft outline of the White Paper has a proposed chapter on this topic. The committee is working openly and papers for NAGCELL can be found on the DfEE's lifelong learning website. David Blunkett, the Secretary of State for education, has talked of 'turning the oil tanker around' as a metaphor in relation to slowly changing the direction of education for the better. If this can work for all adults in relation to learning, surely it will benefit those with mental health difficulties as well?

◼ KEY THEMES AND ISSUES

- Funding from a variety of sources is necessary to meet the overall requirements of people with mental health difficulties. A multi-agency approach is needed to put together appropriate packages of services.

- Each source of funding has specific criteria and constraints attached.

- An effective funding strategy:
  - ◼ recognises that students often need extended pre-entry advice and guidance as well as ongoing support
  - ◼ has flexibility to accommodate periods of interrupted learning
  - ◼ recognises that some students need longer to achieve their learning goals
  - ◼ allocates resources to specialist staff for liaison and non-teaching activities, in order to provide support and to make links with their colleagues in other agencies, developing effective collaborative working relationships
  - ◼ works in partnership with other service providers to avoid duplication or gaps
  - ◼ recruits specialist staff with status and authority to be effective across the organisation and outside it
  - ◼ makes a commitment to provision and achieves stability and continuity of provision to minimise students' uncertainty and anxiety

◼ QUESTIONS

- Do you have a funding strategy which utilises funding from a variety of sources?

- Has your organisation given a commitment to explore other sources of funding? If so, which?

- Are you aware of the eligibility criteria and constraints of each source of funding?

- Does your resource allocation mechanism allow for staff to liaise with colleagues from other organisations to develop effective working relationships?

- How can you seek to ensure stability of funding and continuity of provision?

- How can you ensure that programmes for students with mental health difficulties are determined by learners' needs and not by accreditation requirements?

CHAPTER EIGHT

GETTING IN: ACCESS, GUIDANCE AND ASSESSMENT

I f more people with mental health difficulties are to participate in education in the future, then effective outreach and access strategies will be crucial. Getting as far as enrolment is often the most difficult step for someone to take. A positive approach which targets people with mental health difficulties give a clear signal that the organisation is committed to catering for this group of learners. It means being pro-active, not waiting for people to knock on your door!

As the following situation demonstrates, unless there is a pro-active approach and a thorough needs analysis is carried out in the locality, people with mental health difficulties may remain excluded from educational opportunities. A college wrote in response to the questionnaire survey:

> Using your definition of people with mental health difficulties, [this] college does not offer any provision [for people with mental health difficulties] since to date no one has come forward requesting assistance for such problems.

Some people with mental health difficulties will be able to use educational provision without any additional help. Some will choose not to disclose their mental health difficulties at enrolment. The danger in not doing so is that support needs will not have been identified and will not be in place when required. This can result in subsequent drop-out and the experience of failure. Many people will not even get as far as enrolment unless the college or LEA has developed an outreach strategy and appropriate pre-entry guidance and initial assessment procedures. As one college manager wrote:

> The mere thought of entering a large or busy college environment can be simply too much for some students. I have seen one student in tears at the thought of entering our building.

For the potential student with mental health difficulties, the initial 'contact' – which may be meeting someone from the college or LEA face-to-face, picking up a leaflet or seeing a poster – is critical. If an initial meeting is too intimidating or a leaflet makes the course sound too daunting, this can make all the difference between someone saying 'Yes, maybe that's for me', or feeling 'I couldn't possibly do that.'

Anyone developing outreach work needs to consider the following:

- Who are you going to target and how (given that one in four people will have a mental health problem at some point in their life)?
- What kind of information do potential students need and how do you present it?
- What kind of referral system (if any) will operate?

TARGETING POTENTIAL STUDENTS WITH MENTAL HEALTH DIFFICULTIES

When asked how the organisation attempts to identify students with mental health difficulties, the following responses were given. The percentages indicate the proportion of those answering who used each source.

	FE responses to %	*LEA responses to %*
Self-identification	86	68
Referral sources (eg, day centres)	79	82
At the guidance interview	63	50
At an additional support needs interview	58	29
Tutors referring existing students	66	54
Other	12	21

Forging links with mental health services is the most obvious way of making contact with people with mental health difficulties. Many colleges and LEAs have successfully recruited students through informal visits and more formal meetings with staff and potential students at:

- day centres;
- drop-ins;
- group homes
- long-stay hospitals

- day hospitals;
- social clubs;
- hostels;
- secure units.

This has a number of advantages.

- You are giving a clear message that you actively want to recruit learners with mental health difficulties.
- Contact is established in a safe and non-threatening environment.
- Education staff can begin to develop a working relationship with mental health staff;
- People can meet and start getting to know education staff so there is a familiar face when they start a course.
- There is an initial opportunity to assess people as potential learners.
- People can explore without commitment at this stage whether they might join a course or class;
- People can explore options the kind of classes they would like and the subjects they would be interested in learning about.
- Taster courses can be arranged (see below) to help people decide what they might like to do.

Southwark College has developed an effective strategy for outreach work with mental health service users:

> A senior lecturer from Southwark College holds 'advice sessions' every six weeks in day centres and mental health resource centres. These events are well publicised and have helped increase recruitment. There are also termly meetings with senior staff at outreach sites where discrete courses are held to discuss how things are going and see what is and is not working well.

In Nottingham a very focused outreach strategy was adopted:

> An Education Counsellor's post was established in collaboration with a directorate of Mental Healthcare. Initially she was based at one of the day centres which meant she was frequently available and the Centre's users could get to know her on an informal basis. As a result, a lot of their fears about education were broken down and good working relationships were established with all the staff. In effect, a cultural change took place, and although it was still difficult to get users to take the risks involved in going to college, within a year, half of them were going to college and many were confident enough to self-refer. Moreover, the success was seen by other parts of the Mental Healthcare Trust who then started to request similar provision.

REACHING NON-MENTAL HEALTH SERVICE USERS

Many people with mental health difficulties will not be in touch with mental health services. Some may be former users, while others may never have used specialist support. Outreach strategies will need to include ways of reaching people who may not be in touch with any services and who can often be very isolated. To attract people who are not mental health service users, information can be circulated in places such as health centres, libraries, supermarket notice boards, local radio and newspapers, women's drop-ins, hostels, neighbourhood centres and other community settings.

It's important to allow for the 'chance' factor. In one college, two-thirds of the students on a discrete course for people with mental health difficulties had approached the college for 'other reasons'. They had not set out to enrol on the course but had ended up in provision which was meeting their particular needs.

The LIFT project in Leicester has been able to reach people who have mental health difficulties, but who are not using mental health services:

> Recruitment was 'discreet' with the LIFT leaflets being left in the reception area of the college for people to take away. Leaflets were also offered to enquirers who had used the Guidance Service and who might be interested. Within a week or two, enough people had shown an interest for the co-ordinator to see the first group of potential students who included two 'referrals' from outside organisations. Apart from these, all the others self-referred to the college. When they joined the project, more than half were receiving little or no support from mental health services or agencies funded to support people with mental health difficulties.

Including information about discrete provision in the college's or LEA's main prospectus can also help to reach students who may be unsure about whether to use specialist provision, but also carries the message that courses for people with mental health difficulties are seen as part of the overall provision for adult learners. Information about provision for people with mental health difficulties should be included in other general information resources. Colleges and LEAs are also required by the 1995 Disability Discrimination Act to produce disability statements which give details of the provision they make and points of contact (see Appendix C).

Written information

The way information about courses is presented says a lot about how the college or LEA views learners with mental health difficulties. A poster or leaflet with poor layout, spelling mistakes and bad grammar is not going to attract potential learners. As one specialist LEA worker observed: 'Much of what is used does us little credit; it's poorly written, poorly presented and poorly printed. Whatever the resources, there's no excuse for poor English and inappropriate language.'

To 'label' or not? Deciding whether to use phrases like 'mental illness' or 'mental health problems' on publicity material can be tricky and will depend to some extent on the recruitment strategies and groups being targeted. If the wording is too vague, then some potential students may not realise that provision is appropriate for them and may not feel confident about even making an initial enquiry. On the other hand, some people may be deterred from enrolling on a course which uses specific mental health terminology. They may feel 'I don't fit into that category'.

Publicity material needs to include three key messages: the course content, aims and objectives; the kind of people course organisers hope to attract; and how students will be helped to succeed on the course if they do enrol.

In the following examples course information makes it clear that the provision is targeting people with mental health difficulties but does so in a way which, hopefully, potential learners find acceptable.

> **This course is for you if:**
> **you are worried or stressed;**
> **meeting strangers is hard for you;**
> **you have been depressed;**
> **you feel anxious or nervous.**

> **Are you wanting to get into paid work during the next year?**
> **If you are experiencing emotional distress or mental health difficulties**
> **as a result of unemployment or if you have left previous jobs**
> **because of emotional distress/stress**
> **then you could get free help and support**
> **towards employment.**

Although publicity materials do not usually go into any great detail about the kind of support that will be made available, the following kind of statements (from existing publicity materials) can encourage people who are uncertain whether or not to join a class:

> The course takes place in a relaxed atmosphere.
>
> *This course is for people who do not yet feel ready to join a mainstream course.*
>
> We can offer ongoing support and a flexible approach to help you to succeed and this course could help you make a new start.
>
> *Learn at your own pace and in a supportive atmosphere. If you are unsure about enrolling, you can try the subject out for a week or two.*
>
> If you feel unwell and miss a few sessions, don't worry; you'll be welcomed back when you feel ready.

The important messages are:

- we recognise that you may have difficulties with learning;
- you won't be put under pressure;
- but you will be encouraged and helped to succeed;
- we recognise your support needs and will do our best to meet them.

Including the following practical information is also helpful:

Named contact person Whenever possible, publicity material should include a named contact person, giving a telephone number and address including room number and site if the organisation is multi-sited. This can make initial contact with the college less daunting.

Details of fees Knowing that the course is free or has reduced fees will be important for many people with mental health difficulties who are likely to be on benefits. Also information about other costs for materials, visits, etc, needs to be specified.

Location and travel instructions Brief details about the course location and how it can be reached on public transport are also useful. If even getting to college can be daunting and you're uncertain whether you can manage it, having this kind of preliminary information can be reassuring.

And a final point on publicity. What kind of title do you give the course or scheme? Choosing a title with positive connotations is important. Titles like 'Stepping Stones' or 'One Step at a Time' are non-stigmatising and imply progress (but only a step at a time!). Seeking the advice of current or potential students will help to check out the suitability of the title.

Recruiting students through referrals from mental health services or carers

Arrangements vary. Most colleges and LEAs making specialist provision encourage people to make their own applications, with support if they prefer. A few providers will only accept students who have been referred by a mental health professional or family carer.

Asking mental health services to refer potential students has a number of advantages as already mentioned but there are several potential disadvantages. Staff may:

- refer people inappropriately if they are not familiar with what is being provided and who it is suitable for;
- put pressure on someone to enrol on a course, although that is not what the person wants to do;
- refer inappropriately because they want to move someone on from their own service;
- use education provision as a way of freeing up places in mental health day services.

One of the most successful ways of attracting new students is by word of mouth. Staff and students in mental health services will see how adult education has benefited one person and recommend it to other users. More often it is through informal networks of mental health service users, although this will depend on the strength of user networks. Day centre attendance can speed communication, although if people do not talk much to each other, the 'information flow' will be slower. As one college tutor remarked:

> I've noticed a snowballing among our group . . . you persuade someone to come to a class who was very nervous about the idea of going to a college at all . . . after a while they've gone to college and found nothing dire has happened to them and then they tell other people at the day centre who then think 'Yes, perhaps I can do that too.'

People already at college can also be more formal 'ambassadors':

> Students who are mental health service users organise and facilitate open afternoons for people considering enrolment. The students are available to talk about college life and answer questions.

Taster courses

Taster courses can be useful for anyone who is unsure about whether to enrol but are also helpful for people who have already decided to join a class but are unsure which one. Tasters can:

- provide an opportunity for people to get a feel of what adult learning is like;
- give people the chance to try different activities and find out what they want to learn about;
- are ideal for people who find it difficult to make long-term commitments;
- can be held in familiar settings such as day centres or drop-ins;
- can take place on educational sites during the breaks when the atmosphere is less busy and stressful;
- can enable people to get to know a tutor before enrolling on a longer course.

There are various ways of running tasters. Somerset ran a one-day event (Boulton and Hatton, 1991):

The day, for people with mental health difficulties across the county, was held at Bridgwater Arts Centre. After an ice-breaker session, students could choose from five workshops in the morning and a further five in the afternoon. Subjects included science, creative writing, assertiveness and paper marbling. Successful take-up of all subjects indicated that people had a wide range of interests and should not be channelled into a narrow curriculum.

The day was organised very informally with plenty of quiet as well as social space for those wanting time out; although only a few people used the rooms set aside for this it was an important option. Tutors worked flexibly and were prepared for people to move in and out of sessions.

By the end of the day it was clear that people had found it an enjoyable and valued experience and a great deal of learning had taken place. Everyone had felt able to cope and those who found it more difficult were able to opt out as and when they needed to without feeling they would be judged or disapproved of.

...and other access routes

For some people the single biggest barrier to learning may be their difficulty with actually using a college site or other education building. Education staff can encourage people to make informal visits – on their own, with a friend or with the support of a mental health worker, eg, key worker, social worker or community psychiatric nurse. Staff could arrange to meet them at the entrance, take them to the canteen for a coffee perhaps and then show them round the building. This gives them the chance to get a feel for the place without having committed themselves to enrolment or even an advice and guidance session.

Hull College encourages people to come and use their facilities, but without any obligation to enrol:

> College staff regularly send information to the local MIND association and the Community Mental Health Teams telling them about on-campus facilities available to the general public such as hairdressing, beauty treatments, training restaurant and bistro. People with mental health difficulties are encouraged to come into college and use these facilities alongside other members of the public. This allows them to become familiar with the college.

GUIDANCE AND ASSESSMENT

In the survey, we asked colleges and LEAs how they identified potential students with mental health difficulties. In 23.5 per cent of cases, people had identified themselves and about the same proportion were identified by a referrer. For example:

> People are often informed of courses through contact with a community psychiatric nurse, social worker or key worker:
>
> ...through referrals from carers
>
> ...through the psychology unit of the local hospital
>
> where a support agency tells us, but this isn't always disclosed [to the college]

A third of respondents mentioned that guidance interviews or additional support interviews provided an opportunity for identifying mental health difficulties.

However, some colleges and LEAs stated that they had no formal systems for identifying mental health difficulties and assessing their learning support needs:

> No system exists . . .
>
> They are not [assessed]
>
> Very ad hoc
>
> There is no formal referral system nor assessment of their mental health difficulties . . . [but this is] an area currently under review
>
> Mainstream students don't have a formal assessment

When survey respondents were asked about their unmet needs in learning support services, this again was identified as an under-developed area of provision:

> [We] lack trained and qualified staff to provide advice, guidance and counselling.
>
> [We need] more focused guidance and counselling
>
> No appropriate pre-course assessment.
>
> Students' emotional and social needs are not always identified at assessment for vocational courses.

Colleges and LEAs which had structured assessments for identifying the learning support needs of people with mental health difficulties had developed a range of strategies for assessing needs, including:

> individual interviews; diagnostic and screening tests; self-assessments; assessments carried out in conjunction with or by other agencies or services.
>
> personal interview and information from referral agencies plus assessment of basic literacy and numeracy skills

mainly through individual assessment with help, where agreed, from care agencies/health extended advice and guidance interview with member of the Learning Support Team

use of an internally devised assessment based on self-report of where they experience difficulties

individual interview/coffee with the Mental Health Liaison Officer referral to psychiatric services for assessment

assessment by psychology assistant in conjunction with lecturing staff

Effective assessment and guidance are essential if students are to have a positive and enjoyable experience of learning with whatever supports they need to make that happen.

General principles

Our experience is that a great deal of preparatory work is essential if the student is to have an enjoyable and non- threatening experience [of learning]. (FE college)

Developing the right approach to initial guidance and assessment is crucial. It is worth spending some time thinking about the following questions:

- Why are you assessing? (As a 'gatekeeping' measure to protect the organisation? To identify learning and support needs? Both?)
- How do you assess? (Tests? Psychiatric assessments? Interviews? Informal conversations?)
- Where do you assess? (College? Day centre? People's own homes?)
- Who do you need to involve? (Potential students? Carers? Mental health professionals?)
- What do you do with the outcomes of the assessment process?

Whatever system is adopted, arrangements should:

- be flexible and individualised;

- avoid being time-limited;
- explore what the person wants to learn, where and how they would like to learn and how these can best be matched to available options;
- be a mutual process where a potential student can find out if what is being offered is what they want or need;
- directly involve the person at every stage; mental health service users will have had plenty of experiences of other people making judgements about them, testing them, writing reports, etc.
- avoid any messages of 'pass' or 'fail'; people will probably have had many previous experiences of failure;
- focus mainly on the present and the future abilities and aspirations rather than taking a 'case history' approach, except where information about the past is directly relevant.
- seek to facilitate the student's learning in whatever way necessary;
- provide clear explanations as to why questions are being asked;
- provide information about confidentiality;
- ask students how they wish to be helped and who they wish to be involved.

Expectations

Exploring and clarifying expectations should be an integral part of guidance. Potential students need a chance to explore what they might undertake during a course and achieve by the end of it. They need to get an idea of what will be expected from them if they enrol. This can help them decide whether a course is right for them – and whether this is the right time. In other words, this needs to be a mutual process.

The WEST (Work Experience and Skills Training) Project in Leicester aims to develop people's skills and practice so they can move on to further training or into work. Their written information states that they expect trainees 'to meet some of the demands and rigours they would face in the workplace or in further training/education' and suggests that trainees need to be able to meet at least four of the following criteria:

- be interested and motivated to attend training.

- attend at least four out of every five training sessions and be on time.
- be happy learning in groups of between five and ten people.
- be able to travel to the training site or could learn to do this with the project's support within three occasions).
- be motivated to progress on to other opportunities in the future – even if this is difficult to imagine or your self-confidence does not seem high enough at present.

At the LIFT project, guidance is a central element, both before and after students enrol:

> *Before making a 'learning contract' to join the project, individual guidance sessions took place where the aims of the project were explained and discussed...Each [student] had time to re-consider if it was the right thing for them...Although LIFT aimed to support them towards work, it was made clear that job outcomes were not predictable or guaranteed because of the project's open-ended nature and each individual student's situation and choices*
> (GREEN, FORTHCOMING)

Reaching the 'right' decision is not always a straightforward process, as Jenkins (forthcoming) writes:

> *This is one of the most difficult areas of work with people with mental health difficulties. People who are withdrawn and very anxious or, conversely, who are full of almost manic energy and plan a punishing schedule of courses can pose a real dilemma for guidance workers...there is a need for balance between over- protectiveness and a realistic assessment of the demands of a course or courses and the resources of the client.*

Assessment should be identifying students' strengths and interests as well as looking at any potential barriers to learning. Motivation may not always be sufficient, but as one lecturer explained:

> I think I spend most of my time looking for 'sparks of enthusiasm'...I work in education and my passion is enthusiasm; that's what I'm looking for, measuring, assessing. Have they enthusiasm for what they are doing?

WHAT DO YOU NEED TO KNOW?

Requests for information should be on a 'need to know' basis. Getting hold of information will almost certainly be easier if students are told why they are being asked a particular question. There are a number of reasons why potential students may be asked for information about their mental health difficulties. Education providers need to consider the following questions:

- What grounds do they have for asking someone about their behaviour, for example?
- Are they singling out students with mental health difficulties unnecessarily?
- Should the same arrangements be applied to all students?

People with mental health difficulties frequently experience prejudice and discrimination (Read and Baker, 1996) and it is important to remember that:

- there is no evidence that the rate of violence amongst mental health service users is greater than for other citizens;
- the total number of homicides has doubled in the past twenty years but the number of homicides committed by people with mental health difficulties has remained static;
- people with mental health difficulties are more likely to commit suicide than homicide.

Information about a person's mental health should only be requested where it may affect their learning. Requests for psychiatric diagnoses should be avoided. They are not likely to be very helpful to teaching staff as they say nothing about how an individual learns or about the implications of the mental illness for their learning. There is also the danger of evoking negative and inaccurate stereotypes about mental health difficulties. At Croydon Community Education Service:

> People aren't asked for a diagnosis although they may offer one themselves. [We] feel there are too many stereotyped associations around words like 'schizophrenia' which aren't particularly helpful. We are about learning and the learning environment.

Potential students need to know that any information they give will not be used against them but that it is needed to help the college provide a comfortable and appropriate learning programme and environment. At Clarendon College:

> Students may be invited to write a confidential letter to their tutor describing their learning needs. For example, someone might say that they will probably be very anxious for the first few weeks so may not show their true potential but after that they should settle down and be able to keep up with the rest of the class. The letter also makes it clear what the status of the information is and to whom, if anyone it may be passed.

Confidentiality (or 'who needs to know?')

Deciding who should have access to information can be difficult, as these comments from education staff demonstrate:

> If we say too much the student won't be welcomed . . .
>
> . . . if we fail to report a risk and something goes wrong, then we may be considered guilty of neglect.
>
> Many students don't want staff and other students to know of their mental health difficulties.

Because of the stigma commonly associated with mental health difficulties, students may well be concerned about who will have access to information and education providers need to be able to justify their policies on confidentiality and avoid unnecessary discrimination:

> *In general, information on people with mental health difficulties should be collected and dealt with in the same way as with other [students]. Any differences in practice should be examined very carefully and only maintained where there is a clear justification.*
>
> (JENKINS, FORTHCOMING)

Wherever possible, confidentiality agreements should not be broken without the student's permission, although there may occasionally be a need to do so. If a student is becoming very disturbed, for example, and is refusing to seek help of their own accord, it may be necessary for the college to contact an appropriate external agency.

Risk policies and procedures

Unfortunately, media coverage of mental illness tends to focus almost exclusively on aggression and violence, fuelling public concern about safety in the community, even though:

> *Statistically one is far more likely to be attacked or killed by a member of one's own family than by an outsider with mental health difficulties. It should also be acknowledged that emotional and behavioural difficulties, especially where linked to substance abuse, are not the exclusive province of people with mental health difficulties and can be encountered in any situation where someone has a responsibility for dealing with members of the public.*
> (JENKINS, FORTHCOMING)

Only a very small proportion of students with mental health difficulties are likely to pose any risk to staff or other students. As Lancaster's Adult College has found:

In the fourteen years that the College has worked with people with mental health difficulties in the local hospital and in discrete classes, no violent or unacceptably anti-social acts have taken place. This is with up to nineteen classes a week and over the years more than one thousand students with mental health problems. In the four years of our Stepping Stone (county-wide) programme for people with mental health difficulties, with over four thousand enrolments, we have not heard of any aggressive behaviour.

The majority are more likely to be afraid of other people or their own behaviour. Nevertheless, risk assessment policy and practice does need to be addressed:

– who are you going to assess and how?
– what arrangements do you need to deal with crises?

— are there ways of minimising or avoiding crises?

Having identified potential risks, it is important to identify support needs and any necessary precautions which could hopefully minimise the chance of any incidents occurring. Students can be asked how they would like staff to respond and who can be contacted if necessary (eg, key worker, social worker, community psychiatric nurse). One college enrolled 'at risk' students on a part-time basis on an agreed contract and gradually built up their attendance.

Risk assessment should not focus solely on the individual student. An inclusive learning approach means creating a learning environment which is responsive to the needs of all potential students. For example:

- organising training programmes for teaching staff but also for front-line staff in reception, libraries, canteens, etc. A confident response by a staff member may defuse or prevent an incident.
- finding ways of creating a less stressful environment. Anyone can experience rising levels of tension or anger in a stressful environment;
- drawing up (and regularly updating) a list of relevant telephone numbers of people who can be contacted in an emergency (eg, social services duty team; mental health crisis team).

■ KEY THEMES AND ISSUES

- a proactive approach is needed, based on a thorough needs analysis of the locality, if people with mental health difficulties are to be enabled to participate in education

- the language and style of publicity materials can be crucial in attracting potential students

- some people with mental health difficulties will choose not to disclose their mental ill health

- the initial guidance and assessment process is essential in ensuring that students undertake appropriate learning programmes matched to their requirements and that their support needs are identified and provided from the outset

- the criteria for admissions to courses and any selection procedures need to be made explicit and the expectations of students and demands upon them need to be clarified

- organisations need to develop policy and practice on confidentiality which balance the need to know with respect for individual privacy

■ QUESTIONS

- Do you have a range of outreach strategies to contact potential students locally? How effective are they? Have you identified all of the local organisations for people with mental health difficulties? Do you have effective links with them? How widely available is your publicity material? In libraries, supermarket notice boards, doctors surgeries etc?

- Is your publicity material of the same quality and standard as all college material? Have you considered the language to use and have you checked them with mental health service users?

- Does your publicity material include:
    - ■ course aims, objectives and content?
    - ■ the kind of people the course hopes to attract?
    - ■ how students will be helped to succeed if they enrol?
    - ■ name telephone number & location of a contact person?
    - ■ details of any fees, charges or expenses?
    - ■ location and travel information?

CHAPTER NINE

STAYING THE COURSE: SUPPORT FOR LEARNING

If we're not able to tailor support to meet individual needs, then we're disabling learning.
(HUXLEY, 1993)

We can't do the course for them, but we can make it easier"
(STAFF MEMBER, COMMUNITY COLLEGE)

For people with mental health difficulties to have an enabling – rather than – disabling – experience of education, pre- and post-enrolment support needs to be available as a 'seamless service'.

Pre-enrolment learning support for an individual can include: pre-entry guidance, visits to college, meetings with tutors, exchange of information. Post-enrolment support could involve any or all the following: counselling, learning support, befriending support; peer support.

Access to appropriate support right from the start can make all the difference between whether someone has a positive experience of education or not. A key element of pre-entry guidance and counselling will include a thorough assessment of learning support needs and the drawing up of an action plan setting out how the identified needs will be met. The importance of this is recalled by a student's description of a meeting he had with the college worker and his key worker:

> The three of us met at the day centre for an informal chat. I have always regarded that meeting as a vital link in my progression towards college life. For the [college staff member] to come in and have a meeting with me and the key worker and have the knowledge to put the discussion together into an Action Plan was something that none of us could have achieved alone. The college staff member and my key worker seemed happy to co-operate on my behalf, each offering her own special area of knowledge and skills, with no sense of competition or professional jealousy.

The experiences of students and staff in colleges and LEAs which have developed provision for people with mental health difficulties suggest that good support is:

- available when needed by the student;
- offers a choice of how that support is delivered;
- builds on people's abilities, strengths and capacities;
- avoids or minimises inappropriate dependence;
- flexible and responsive to individual needs;
- delivered through a wide range of strategies;
- can respond to crises as well as ongoing needs;
- is provided in ways which are non-stigmatising;
- is based on individual students' needs and negotiated with them;
- is reliable and consistent: 'professional' in the best sense;
- is clear about what is (and is not) being offered by way of support;
- is able to support people from pre-entry, during a course and through progression to other activities;
- uses people's natural (existing) supports wherever possible;
- does not see people solely in terms of their diagnosis or 'mental health difficulties';
- provides opportunities for people to share with others who face similar struggles;
- enables students to develop coping strategies.

Most education providers are aware that their support services for people with mental health difficulties are not well developed. Our survey asked colleges and LEAs how they rated their support of students with mental health difficulties.

Only one in twenty described their learning support services for this group as 'well developed' and just over half described them as inadequate. Typical responses indicated that learner support was:

> ad hoc and not well planned
>
> patchy...
>
> not systematically addressed...many unmet needs [we] lack a formal commitment to such groups

Lack of priority in funding for this work and lack of staff with the necessary expertise to undertake this work were cited as reasons:

> No suitably trained or experienced staff
>
> [Lack of] a named person with specific experience...outside our current budget
>
> [Lack of] time and bodies to give individual support in the learning environment...funding is totally insufficient
>
> We need more support assistants and additional tutorial time
>
> [Need] more financial and personal support for students in mainstream provision.

SUPPORT...FOR LEARNING

Adult and further education is about learning and takes place in a learning environment. It is not about 'treatment' or 'therapy' which are provided by other agencies and which people with mental health difficulties may need to access elsewhere. Support should reflect this. Arrangements need to focus on what individuals require in order to be able to learn effectively.

Establishing some clear boundaries will be important. Someone embarking on a course for the first time may expect the same kind of support as a day centre offers, particularly if they are using discrete provision. Support needs to maintain a balance which acknowledges a person's mental health difficulties and their potential impact on learning, but also recognises that people are learners or students, not 'clients' or 'patients'. A key aim of education is to ensure that students learn to take responsibility for their learning. For example:

> *Once [students] had officially started on a course, the emphasis was on them accepting responsibility for attendance and their own learning agreements with tutors in specific workshops, at the same time as being supported by tutorials from the Guidance Team.*
> (GREEN, FORTHCOMING)

Individual needs vary but a person may need support in the following areas:

- getting to a class (eg, making sure someone gets up in the morning; support with travel and going into a college building);
- support in the classroom (eg, if someone needs to leave the room or is having difficulty with a particular task);
- learning support outside classes (eg, help with completing assignments or support with developing particular skills);
- opportunities for review, problem-solving and general support; for learning (eg, helping someone return after an absence).

Having a range of support strategies will be helpful so that individual support requirements can be met. At Southwark College, for example:

> A range of support is available to students with mental health difficulties on mainstream courses. This includes: help with transport, informal drop-in sessions, weekly sessions with the college counselling staff and additional specialist support. Individual students can access any or all of these depending on their particular needs.

Support can be provided by a range of people including:

- specialist staff (eg, guidance team; learning support team)
- support tutors
- support assistants
- course tutors
- volunteers/befrienders as learning partners or in a similar supportive role;

    — other students with mental health difficulties;

    — the organisation's counselling service;

    — staff from other organisations (eg, key workers, care workers).

In addition, receptionists, office staff, canteen staff and other non-teaching staff can sometimes provide an invaluable source of informal support, even though they do not usually have a designated support role in the organisations. This informal support has often proved crucial.

In our survey, some similarities but also clear differences emerged in the provision of support between FE colleges and local education authorities, as the following table shows:

	Proportion of respondents providing support (%)	
	FE colleges	LEAs
Guidance and counselling	81	80
Learning support assistants	78	48
Additional tutor support	76	48
Time for additional tutoring	57	36
Social work support	31	65
Health service support	27	56
Transport support	27	44
Drop-ins	15	28
Buddy/mentoring schemes	–	56
Peer group support	–	36

The provision of guidance and counselling is consistent in about 80 per cent of FE colleges and LEAs. In FE colleges, most support is provided by the college's own guidance and support staff, tutors and learning support assistants, whereas in LEA provision there is greater use of social work and health service support and buddy or mentoring schemes. Support with transport is more frequently provided as is peer group support. These differences may reflect funding differences. Organisations can claim resources for additional support for FEFC-funded courses whereas LEA funding does not have this facility and other means of support have been developed.

According to our survey, support was most frequently provided by guidance and counselling staff, learning support assistants and teaching staff. For many students, the provision of ongoing support will greatly increase their chances of 'staying the course'. Experience has shown that there are particular times when access to support can be especially helpful.

- During the first few weeks of a course: this might involve a person's key worker travelling with them to college; or someone from the learning support team meeting them at the entrance and accompanying them to the classroom; or weekly one-to-one guidance sessions.

- Around holidays and breaks: when someone may feel very isolated, may have difficulty in managing without the structure of a course or may relapse. Collaboration with other organisations may be needed to set up some additional support.

- At the point of moving from a course provided in a mental health setting such as a day centre to a class on a college site or other education setting: if members of the same class and their tutor move together this can make the transition less stressful.

- When a student moves from discrete provision onto a mainstream course: regular guidance sessions or classroom support may be appropriate when someone loses the support of peers in a discrete class.

- Before and/or during an exam or assessment: additional tutor support or peer support may be helpful. It may also be necessary to negotiate special arrangements with the assessing body early on in the course.

- When there are unforeseen changes: eg, tutor absence; new tutor at short notice; change of venue – when support from someone familiar to the students can reduce anxiety.

- Towards the end of a class or course and in preparing for progression when there may uncertainty about next steps, and loss of a peer support network, etc.

Learning support on FEFC-funded provision may be claimed through completion of a form for additional support units, whereas non-Schedule-2 provision – often run by LEAs – usually relies on volunteers or befrienders. Some schemes offer a free place for anyone supporting a learner with mental health difficulties. In some instances, the Mental Illness Specific Grant has been used to fund support by befrienders.

Volunteers/befrienders

Where volunteers provide support it is important that they are carefully selected, briefed, trained and supported. Bolton Community Education Service offers an accredited training for volunteers:

> The CES runs a volunteer training course for people who may be interested in supporting students with mental health problems or learning difficulties within the Service's classes. The course is accredited through the Greater Manchester Open College Federation.

Having a designated staff member responsible for work with volunteers can help ensure that work is well organised and that students and volunteers are properly supported. Development funds can sometimes be obtained for this:

> Warrington Collegiate Institute has obtained LEA Development Fund monies, enabling them to recruit a part-time volunteer co-ordinator whose role will include recruiting volunteers, organising their training and matching them with students. The main focus will be on supporting students in discrete provision and supporting them in the transition into mainstream provision

Volunteers or befrienders can support students in different ways, both in the classroom and elsewhere and it is important that everyone involved is clear about what is being offered. Clarendon College uses a contract system:

The College recruits befrienders through the local Volunteer Bureau. The college offers initial training and ongoing support to the volunteers who may accompany a student to classes or help them get to the classroom or meet up in breaks and go with them to the canteen. After student and befriender have had time to get to know one another, a contract is drawn up, setting out the agreed commitment.

Staff from other services providing support

In some colleges and LEAs, staff from mental health services or social services accompany students on courses. They may either enrol together and be a learning partner or be there as a non-student, providing informal support but not participating directly in classroom activities. Other service staff need to approach this with sensitivity and an awareness that they are 'wearing another hat'.

Some students may not be comfortable with this arrangement. On the other hand, having a mental health professional as a learning partner has enabled some people with potentially alienating behaviours to enrol on mainstream courses when this would otherwise have been difficult.

Support assistants

The learning (or classroom) support assistant can be invaluable in facilitating an individual student's learning and enabling them to cope with the college environment. Learning support services will need to consider what particular kinds of support are likely to be needed by students with mental health difficulties.

South Nottingham College has considerable experience with providing classroom support for students with physical disabilities or visual impairments. Support for students with mental health difficulties has been introduced more recently and the service is still developing. Using feedback from students who are mental health service users, they have drawn up a list of tips for support assistants (which would be equally useful for volunteers and befrienders). Students suggest that support staff should:

- be fully aware of their role, in and outside the classroom;
- be aware of the wide variety of mental health conditions;

- avoid stereotypes and incorrect perceptions about mental health service users;
- be able to take notes;
- assume that the student has some degree of intelligence and because their condition affects memory or concentration this does not mean they are stupid;
- have an appreciation of differing teaching approaches;
- be sensitive to the student's feelings at any given time;
- be able to anticipate and act to avoid difficulties (eg, interposing themselves between the supported student and a situation they find threatening to an appropriate degree, ie, a student may feel better able to cope at some times than others);
- be an enabler: in sensing the student's needs the support worker must be able to withdraw sensitively as appropriate enabling the student to develop confidence and skills;
- be aware of what is going on in the rest of the class;
- have a calm relaxed approach and be 'unfazed';
- be able to take the student back through what has been discussed or taught, breaking it down step by step.

Unhelpful strategies are the 'opposites' of the above list with the following addition:

- It is unhelpful to adopt a condescending and patronising attitude. This might involve statements such as 'You're not going to let that beat you are you?, implying an element of 'own fault' and childishness on the student's part. Also referring to the student as 'dear', taking over too much and thus not being an enabler.

These 'tips' are one of a series of guidelines on learner support produced by the College and updated regularly in the light of experience. Training for all support staff is obligatory and is supplemented by written materials including these guidelines. Accreditation for training for support assistants is available and is increasingly being taken up.

Peer support

The help which students give each other is one of the most effective forms of support. A great deal of this support happens on an informal basis. For example:

> Carol and Sue are both on the Work Skills Project based at Peterborough Adult Education College in Cambridgeshire. Prior to attending college they had both undertaken a work preparation course at Centre 17. They feel that coming to college together helped them make the transition successfully.

Sometimes two or more students will arrange to meet up and travel to college together so that they can support each other.

Students often emphasise the importance of being in classes with people who have shared similar experiences. People listen to one another, offer support, help each other understand more about their difficulties, and use their collective experiences for problem-solving, as these students have found:

> We've got different sorts of people in our college and they're all in the same boat; and we talk about our problems and mix and mingle and try to overcome the problems...why we're going wrong, what made us do what we did in the first place, how we ended up in this place, how we can change things that will make it better. The most important part is that we're...in the same boat. In this place we can talk about it...a common problem.
>
> I enjoyed being part of a group who accepted me for me and who I could be totally honest with regarding my situation.
>
> You often find people frightened to speak out – but give them the opportunity and they'll take it. Our meetings are such an opportunity. And we can give each other a pat on the back for what we've managed to achieve.

Some schemes have set up groups whose functions may include self-help, mutual support and advocacy. The LIFT project, for example:

has a Self-Help Group which meets for two to three hours each week. The group includes current LIFT students plus one or two students from the previous year who are not in work and who, after some induction, have taken on a befriending role with new students. The group can offer a safe environment for discussing individual and mutual difficulties. The formal meeting is sometimes followed by trouble-shooting sessions with the Project Co-ordinator, either one-to-one or in small groups for any issues which need swift resolution. Group members also have the chance to take on tasks such as taking the minutes, enabling them to develop new skills in a safe environment.

■ KEY THEMES AND ISSUES

- effective learning support systems:
  - ■ offer a range of strategies for providing support, matched to individual students' requirements
  - ■ identify support needs at the earliest opportunity and make timely delivery of support
  - ■ provide support which empowers students and decreases dependency

- effective support can make all the difference to successful learning

- learning and practical support is provided by a wide range of staff, both formally and informally and includes those without a designated support role such as reception and office staff

- if volunteers give support, they need to be carefully selected, briefed, trained and supported.

- peer and self support strategies are valuable and encourage independence

- staff from within education and from other agencies may provide aspects of support. It is essential to be clear about their specific roles and responsibilities and to provide guidance on using support

■ QUESTIONS

- Do you have a support service which operates pre-entry, on course and at exit or through progression? Who is the senior manager responsible for support?

- Do students have a choice on how their support is delivered? Does the support build on students' existing or natural supports? Is support individually negotiated and monitored? Does it encourage students to become more independent an to develop coping strategies?

- Are all the partners involved in the support process – tutors, support staff and students – clear about what support is on offer? Are they all involved in evaluation?

- Are all staff in the organisation aware of the ways in which they may formally or informally provide support? Are support staff from external organisations and volunteers fully aware of their role?

- What forms of support are available for staff and others providing support? Are they fully aware of where and how they can obtain support for themselves?

CHAPTER TEN

GETTING ON...MOVING ON: ACCREDITATION AND PROGRESSION

...progression has to be looked at from two angles. First, it is a personal achievement to actually present oneself at college in the hope that a place that professes to serve the community, regardless of race, sex, age, religion or disability, means what it says. Second, progression can also be at an academic level where opportunities are opened up and maintained.

(BRAILSFORD, 1993: 14)

Some people have been so ill that a tiny bit of progress is really something – a milestone.

(COLLEGE LECTURER)

How do we go about the process of measuring the 'progress' and achievements of adult learners with mental health difficulties? As NIACE has suggested, it is not a straightforward matter, and there are dimensions which are not necessarily quantifiable but nevertheless important indicators of progress:

For people with a long-term mental illness, defining progress can be problematic... For some, the growth of social skills, confidence and re-established relationships may be more crucial than the development of skills and knowledge more easily measured.

(NIACE, 1994: PARA 24)

Further education defines 'progression' in terms of moving from one programme to another. Progress for a student with mental health difficulties needs to be measured against individual learning plans and targets which have been set.

In all cases, progress and achievement need to be recognised, whether through qualifications, part-qualifications, or other outcomes. As with other learners, progression for each individual will be about moving from one learning programme to another and increasing the demands made on them.

Progress for a student with mental health difficulties may include:

- enrolling in a class following a 'taster' or brief introductory course;
- moving from a class in a day centre to discrete provision in an educational setting;
- progressing from a discrete course to mainstream FE or AE provision;
- moving from a smaller building onto the main campus;
- starting an Access to Higher Education course;
- progression within a course such as starting a work placement.

The outcomes of successful learning and achievement may be demonstrated by:

- becoming a volunteer, befriender or advocate;
- doing (unpaid) work experience;
- getting a job;
- developing a more independent lifestyle;
- moving out of supported accommodation;
- having better mental health.

The outcomes for individuals on a course will be different as the following experiences demonstrate. They can involve improved skills for independent living or progression to a range of other educational opportunities (see next page).

CURRENT CHALLENGES

Inclusive Learning (FEFC, 1996) and *Learning Works* (FEFC, 1997) were both concerned with making education more accessible to people who were currently under-represented. Progression and achievement is a central issue.

Provision needs to be sufficiently flexible to allow for periods of interrupted learning which will be unavoidable for some people who have recurrent episodes of mental distress. Programmes which have a modular or unit structure will enable learners to take part of a course, even if they do not manage the whole of it.

The Community Education Service in Coventry has been working with twelve adults living in supported accommodation. The OCN-accredited Communication through Craft course included modules on craft, personal development, group work, organisation and management skills. Since undertaking the course:

– one person now co-tutors (with the course tutor) at a home for the elderly and has independently set up craft sessions at another home;

– two people have enrolled in basic maths and English classes;

– three people have enrolled in computer classes;

– two people have undertaken an ESOL course;

– eight are doing GCSE Art which will increase their potential to develop a craft project, self-employment or set up a co-operative;

– one person has moved to independent living.

The STEP pre-vocational and training programme is run by the Training and Vocational Guidance Service of North Birmingham Mental Health Trust. Progression from STEP is tailored to individuals' needs and wishes. Trainees to date have moved on to:

– voluntary work;

– supported part-time vocational training;

– mainstream college courses;

– open learning;

– sheltered therapeutic employment;

– college access courses;

– supported college courses.

It is also important to avoid setting people up to fail by setting goals which are too large or too far ahead. Enabling people to obtain part-qualifications rather than assuming from the start that the will achieve the whole qualification will be essential for some people.

The current interpretation of progression by the FEFC(E) tends to be 'vertical'. People are expected to move on – and up – vocationally or academically. This can be inappropriate where someone's learning requirements may be that they reclaim lost skills, maintain existing skills or prevent further decline.

The FEFC's *Learning Works* report (1997) proposed the establishment of a 'lifetime learning service'. This would have particular relevance for people with longstanding mental health difficulties for whom paid employment may not be a realistic option. Continuing access to a variety of educational opportunities could provide a stimulating alternative to traditional day opportunities for mental health service users and widen their choice.

For some individuals, embarking on a course will mean having to revise their expectations about the future. Becoming a volunteer or finding work of a less demanding nature than previously anticipated can be a painful reminder of the long-term impact of their mental health difficulties. Aspirations have to be balanced by setting realistic and achievable goals, as this student found when working on job applications:

> [It was] very frustrating, knowing the bottom line; ie, I can only do fairly low-paid jobs.

Achieving a balance between setting targets which encourage people to progress but also enable them to do so at their own rate is a challenge. Too much pressure and people may drop out, too little and they may feel they are going nowhere. Targets need to be realistic and achievable with clear, short-term landmarks to work towards. The length of a course may suit one person but not another and course design is not always sufficiently flexible to allow for these differences, though in some cases, it is possible to repeat parts. However, if students don't move on, this can seriously restrict opportunities for new students to join.

It was clear from the survey that the issue of progression was not always being addressed at a strategic level. Discrete provision had been established, but progression routes had not been identified, developed or properly resourced, either within the organisation or in collaboration with other agencies. As a college staff member pointed out, students may be given the message: 'we'll help you as long as you don't get well'. Without opportunities to move on, there is a danger of creating unnecessary dependence on specialist provision. A full range of learning programmes designed to promote progression and support for all programmes is required.

A number of survey respondents mentioned the lack of opportunities for students to move into mainstream, onto vocational courses or into employment:

> Discrete provision is very supportive. The challenge is how to wean people from discrete provision – and from a tutor. We try and avoid people spending more than two years with just one tutor because we feel that encourages too much dependence. It can end up that college is that tutor.

The process of moving people on from the relatively sheltered environment of a class for people with mental health difficulties and with a known tutor needs to be carefully structured. Employing the same tutor for mainstream and discrete classes can help students make the transition to using general provision:

> The Adult College Lancaster runs yoga/relaxation classes in the local secure unit, in an acute psychiatric unit, and discrete and mainstream classes are available in the college. The same tutor runs all of these weekly classes which allows for a clear progression route for students recovering from an episode of mental ill-health. The college also uses mainstream vocational tutors in six of its seven weekly discrete classes to aid and encourage progression.

WAYS FORWARD

Despite the challenges outlined above, strategies are being developed to address some of the current difficulties with accreditation and progression facing people with mental health difficulties. Nationally there is an interest in examining the qualifications framework to make it more flexible and allow for modular delivery and a credit-based accreditation system. Recommendations by the Tomlinson Committee (FEFC, 1996), if accepted by the FEFC, should lead to positive changes.

Current developments include the following:

- accreditation of discrete courses through the Open College Networks which credit learning in informal and community-based settings.
- Certificates of Attendance and/or Achievement which offer informal recognition.
- a new National Record of Achievement.
- portfolios.

To conclude, the curriculum for students with mental health difficulties needs to:

- be included within overall planning, promote progression and be effectively resourced;
- address individual needs and aspirations;
- be responsive to the particular problems with learning which people with mental health difficulties may experience;
- adopt a holistic approach which values and recognises achievement in terms of academic and vocational needs but also acknowledges developments in other areas of people's lives as legitimate learning outcomes;
- take account of lateral as well as vertical progression;
- attract funding which recognises these issues.

■ KEY THEMES AND ISSUES

- progress and achievement needs to be recognised and to be measured against individual learning plans and targets, which may include personal life skills outcomes as well as academic or vocational ones

- successful outcomes of learning not represented through accreditation may include progression to a more demanding learning programme, leading a more independent life style, becoming a volunteer or undertaking paid or unpaid work

- programmes with a modular or unitised structure are more likely to be able to accommodate patterns of interrupted learning

- setting realistic, short term targets enhances the chances of success

- learning requirements to reclaim lost skills, maintain existing skills or prevent further decline of skills are inconsistent with current interpretations of schedule 2 for FEFC funding

- the development of lifelong learning encompassing a wider range of learning is likely to improve access to education for people with mental health difficulties

- curriculum planning needs to ensure that there are better progression opportunities for students with mental health difficulties than are currently available

- encouraging progression requires carefully planned and structured learning programmes and effective support

■ QUESTIONS

- How do you recognise and measure the progress and achievement of students with mental health difficulties?

- Are your learning programmes flexible enough to allow for periods of interrupted learning? Do you have systems for recognising small amounts of achievement?

- How do you record achievement? How do you record learning outcomes which are not externally accredited?

- Do you negotiate learning goals which are realistic and achievable with short term landmarks against which to monitor progress?

- How do you encourage students to have aspirations which are realistic but which still set an appropriate level of challenge?

- How at senior management level is responsible for the curriculum developments for people with mental health difficulties?

- Do you have a full range of learning opportunities available to students with mental health difficulties? Is your provision designed to promote progression?

- How do you structure the transition from the sheltered environment of a specially designed class through to full use of the organisations curriculum?

CHAPTER ELEVEN

STAFF DEVELOPMENT AND TRAINING

High levels of knowledge, skills, experience and confidence on the part of staff are essential if the further education sector is to become more inclusive.
(FEFC, 1996: 3)

For inclusive learning to become a reality for people with mental health difficulties, colleges, LEAs and other adult education providers must themselves be learning organisations. Staff should be offered a range of training and development opportunities which will enable them to become confident and competent in meeting the needs of students with mental health difficulties, whether they are using specially designed or general provision.

A TRAINING AND DEVELOPMENT STRATEGY

There are currently wide variations in practice, ranging from relatively well developed staff training and development programmes to voluntary attendance at occasional, ad hoc training events. However, the recently-announced Inclusive Learning Quality Initiative to develop a national staff development programme (FEFC, 1997a) should result in significant improvements.

A 'whole college' or LEA approach to training and development can be an effective way of putting mental health onto everyone's agenda. It gives a clear message that mental health is not the sole concern of a small number of staff but concerns everyone. As one specialist worker remarked: 'There's only so much we can do...we can't do everything!' Staff training and development events can communicate that the organisation sees this as an important area of work to which it is committed.

A comprehensive training and development strategy based on a thorough analysis of need will have to address the requirements for all staff including:

- senior managers;
- administrative staff;
- frontline staff (eg, receptionists, library staff, caretakers and canteen workers);
- part-time and full-time teaching staff in mainstream provision;
- part-time and full-time teaching on discrete courses;
- learning support staff (including volunteers and befrienders);
- staff with specific responsibility for student services (eg, tutorials, admissions);
- personal tutors, counsellors and pastoral staff.

It is important to ensure that all staff are aware of their responsibilities for meeting the needs of all students, including those with mental health difficulties. Support needs to be available within the organisation for this. Working with students with mental health difficulties should not be viewed as an option but as integral to an inclusive approach.

An overall strategy can also provide a systematic framework for ongoing training and development activities, rather than one-off days or *ad hoc* sessions. Respondents to our national survey identified a number of weaknesses in their training and development opportunities. The following comments highlight a lack of priority on the part of senior management and the absence of a coherent training and development strategy.

> We have induction training for new tutors, but there is little funding for subsequent training.
>
> Staff are allowed to attend external events but payment for cover is difficult.
>
> ...occasional in-house training for support staff

> When there has been adequate funding we have provided in-house staff and development and access to workshops run by mental health professionals.
>
> Need for mental health awareness training for mainstream staff has been identified but staff are already overworked and cannot commit themselves to more.

Training and development needs will vary (see below) and staff working directly with people with mental health difficulties will need more in-depth input, but recognition that it is a 'whole organisation' responsibility can lessen the isolation and potential marginalisation which specialist staff can experience: feeling 'it's all down to me'.

Since the incorporation of FE colleges, some of the previous local authority cross-college support networks have weakened or disappeared completely, so any other opportunities for staff to meet together for training and development will also help to lessen their isolation. Working with people with mental health difficulties can be stressful and difficult, and bringing staff together whether for training, consultation or other development activities can have an important supportive function. The Community Education Service in Oxford has recently established a network which will:

> meet termly and give staff at all levels the chance to share experiences, find out about sources of information and support and participate in drawing up guidelines for supporting students with mental health difficulties. Topics for meetings will include: presentation and discussion of some case studies based on experience of students with mental health problems; setting personal boundaries; safety issues; identifying good practice; improving access to courses for students who lack confidence; looking after yourself.

The following example is from a work rehabilitation agency, which provides a good example of a training strategy which seeks to create a learning organisation and involves staff, managers and volunteers:

RESTORE is a work rehabilitation scheme for people with mental health problems in a structured and supportive environment. A training strategy, aimed at creating a learning organisation, identifies targets for staff, workers (users), volunteers and the management committee. The aim is for each staff member to spend 5 per cent of their working time on training and development activities. Elements of the strategy are as follows:

- an annual planning day is held when organisational goals are set for the following year;
- the Training and Development worker facilitates training throughout the organisation, based on research into needs;
- all staff can develop vocational rehabilitation skills, with an emphasis on assessment and goal setting;
- training in mental health awareness and dealing with challenging behaviour is provided for all for new staff and volunteers (and the latter are also offered training in the principles of psychiatric vocational rehabilitation;
- staff visit two other rehabilitation projects each year; they are encouraged to attend relevant conferences and feedback from these to colleagues;
- management committee training is held which aims to increase members' awareness of organisational issues and their responsibilities in relation to them.

Volunteers or befrienders (see Chapter Nine) are a valuable resource for learning support services but they also offer ordinary members of the community the opportunity to befriend and support other citizens who happen to have mental health difficulties. Training and support can enable them to work more confidently and sensitively. The Adult Education Service in Northamptonshire has set up a special training course for these volunteers:

The original course and course manual were developed for volunteers supporting people in adult education. That remains the focus but participants now include people from MIND and other voluntary groups which the organisers feel enhanced the work. Open College accreditation is being sought. There are three modules: five taught sessions on disability, equal opportunities and interpersonal skills; practical support of a person for at least ten hours and recorded in a diary system; and five sessions, with invited speakers, on specific disability issues.

The focus of training and development

Training and development must address the identified concerns of staff since they are more likely to participate if it is seen as relevant. This also makes the best use of available resources. The recently-announced FEFC staff development programme will hopefully lead to more training and development being provided, but it is still likely to remain a relatively scarce resource for many organisations.

Mental health matters are often addressed within the context of training on broader issues such as disability awareness, equal opportunities or learning support. This is borne out by the following comments from survey respondents:

> . . . [addressed] indirectly through Adult Basic Education or special needs training
>
> . . . part of awareness-raising package for Learning Difficulties and Disability of Curriculum Manager

A staff development programme can include broader issues, followed by more focused events as the following example demonstrates:

> a series of whole-college introductory training days on learner support were held. Six two-hour sessions on supporting learners with mental health difficulties were held subsequently and were attended by over one hundred staff. These were followed by a series of one-off training sessions targeting specific staff groups including Student Services and Administration.

General training on disability issues or equal opportunities can be helpful in raising awareness. It can also reinforce the point that adult learners share much in common with other students such as adult returners.

However, if education providers are committed to increasing participation by people with mental health difficulties then it will be necessary to address more specific issues. All staff need a basic awareness but staff likely to have direct contact with students with mental health difficulties will need to consider issues such as classroom practice. Managers responsible for people with mental health difficulties will also need specialist training tailored to the particular needs of their post.

In terms of an overall approach, training programmes need to:

- focus on the learning environment and learning needs;
- equip staff with relevant skills and knowledge;
- enable staff to identify networks of support;
- reduce the potential isolation of specialist staff.

Training needs to address the professional concerns of staff but must also seek to increase awareness of their own mental health needs. As this lecturer commented:

> ...the single most effective staff development over the last six years has been an exercise which leads to people considering their own mental health. After this, the students aren't 'them' any more and we are all 'us'. This leads to a much more relaxed, confident and normal approach.

The specific issues which staff will want to address in training and development will depend on their individual circumstances – on their needs, on the kind of provision being made and the students being taught. Two surveys (Boulton and Hatton, 1991; Leach, 1996) aimed at staff in adult and community education services suggested that the following are the kinds of issues which training can usefully address:

- increased general awareness of mental health difficulties;
- exploration of one's own fears and prejudices;
- how to establish a positive learning environment (eg, handling feedback)
- how to design, deliver and evaluate individual learning programmes;
- team building in multi-agency groups;
- skills needed to manage one person but also meet the needs of the rest of the group;
- how to work with volunteers and befrienders providing support in the classroom;
- counselling skills.

Frameworks for training and development

Staff training and development on mental health issues, as we have seen, is often delivered through in-house training programmes. Some staff were also following externally accredited training courses such as City and Guilds Courses 7321 (Learner Support) and 7402 (Counselling and Guidance Skills). Some in-house training is also accredited through the Open College Networks.

One or two survey respondents also mentioned that staff were attending university courses such as the University Certificate in Teaching Students with Special Needs (Durham) and the Certificate in Mental Health Care (Manchester).

Action Learning Sets were also mentioned where up to eight people, plus a facilitator, meet regularly. Individual set members bring a project or issue they want to work on. Participants offer support, information and any other help.

In addition to workshops, seminars and other training events, staff were being supported and helped to develop their knowledge and skills in supervision and/or consultation. For example:

- one-to-one support sessions, held as and when needed;
- informal drop-in sessions for problem-solving on specific issues or about individual students;
- college staff can get advice on specific students from members of the local mental health team;
- monthly supervision with a psychotherapist for staff who run a specialist course;
- case discussion groups;
- regular supervision sessions with the college counsellor;
- visits to other organisations to consult with their staff and learn from their experiences.

Supervision is well established amongst mental health professionals such as counsellors and social workers. Although less common in education, it can be invaluable for key staff working with students with mental health difficulties. It can be an excellent source of support, and the need for regular supervision in what is often very emotionally demanding work should not be underestimated.

Users as trainers

An increasing number of people with mental health difficulties are now offering training and consultancy to statutory and non-statutory agencies including education services. This partly reflects the growth of national and local user groups. Service providers are also beginning to recognise the powerful and unique contribution that users can make to staff training and development.

The Open University employed two trainers to run a staff workshop. Both had used mental health services and as the workshop report said:

> *Having two experienced trainers who themselves had to combine the need to man-age periods of mental distress with other aspects of their lives, including study, was tremendously enlightening, informative and directly helpful to participants.*
> (OPEN UNIVERSITY, 1996: 2)

Feedback from individual participants concurred:

> *Really important to have users running workshops... The trainers were informa-tive, and having had experience of this field, were very believable and real in what they were saying... Most useful part of the day was the trainers sharing their expe-riences with us.*
> (OPEN UNIVERSITY, 1996: 17)

Although it would appear that only a few colleges and LEAs are using their own students as trainers, more are bringing in external trainers with experience of using mental health services (see Chapter Three).

Multi-agency approaches

Training activities which involve other agencies can be an effective way of strengthening alliances, developing mutual understanding, and demonstrating a tangible commitment to shared working and to learning from and about each other.

Opportunities for staff from different agencies to share their skills and know-ledge can have many benefits as one college lecturer has discovered:

> I've found a lot of willingness on the part of people working with mental health
> services to attend training events and to share skills. This is one of the bonuses of
> collaborative working: if you have a number of people from different disciplines or
> backgrounds who become used to meeting each other, they are often willing to
> share their skills, and you can put together a programme of training inexpensively
> and with additional benefits.

Other learning opportunities

Although training and development is usually delivered in the ways described above, it is worth remembering that learning about mental health takes place in other ways. For example:

- Information about mental health can be disseminated through staff newsletters, handbooks, and other material circulated to staff.
- Forums as diverse as equal opportunities groups, governors meetings, management committees and faculty meetings can all be used to raise issues relating to mental health.
- The approach and attitudes of specialist staff convey messages to the rest of the organisation about people with mental health difficulties and how they are perceived.

■ KEY THEMES AND ISSUES

- there are wide variations in practice in staff training and development

- a comprehensive training and development strategy needs to be based on a thorough needs analysis and to address the requirements of all staff

- local authority staff development and support networks have been weakened since the incorporation of FE colleges

- staff training and development is more likely to be effective if it is seen as having immediate relevance. All staff need a general awareness of mental health issues and those with direct contact or responsibility for coordinating provisions will require more specialist training.

- staff training and development programmes need to: focus on the learning environment and learning needs; equip staff with relevant skills and knowledge; enable staff to identify sources of support and reduce isolation of specialist staff.

- mental health service users offering training and consultancy can make a powerful and unique contribution to staff development and training

■ QUESTIONS

- Do senior managers support a whole-organisation approach to staff training and development?

- Are training and development opportunities provided for all staff on mental health issues?

- Does your staff training and development programme meet the different requirements of staff which may range from general awareness to highly specialist skills and knowledge?

- Do staff with particular responsibilities towards students with mental health difficulties have access to specialist support networks?

- Are there training programmes for volunteers and befrienders as well as teaching and support staff?

- Is the training and development provided accredited?

- Do you undertake collaborative training and development activities with other agencies?

SUMMARY POINTS

■ INCLUSIVE APPROACH

The development of learning opportunities for people with mental health difficulties must be accorded priority by education providers in order to address current unmet needs and significant under-representation, highlighted in the recent major reports *Inclusive Learning* (FEFC, 1996) and *Learning Works* (FEFC, 1997).

■ THE RIGHT TO LEARNING

Mental distress affects people from all walks of life and all intellectual abilities. The full range of educational opportunities should be available to people who experience distress, according to their interests, abilities and aspirations.

■ RAISING AWARENESS

Education should be provided in ways which challenge inaccurate and harmful myths and stereotypes about mental health. Mental health difficulties are an exaggeration of feelings we all experience. Organisational policies and practices should recognise that many adult returners face the same barriers as people with mental health difficulties (eg, lack of confidence, negative previous experiences of education) and will be seeking the same benefits – a better quality of life, greater self-confidence and enhanced skills.

■ STUDENT-CENTERED APPROACHES

Educational opportunities should be based on what people with mental health difficulties say they want and need from education. Users should be involved in all aspects of provision to ensure that educational opportunities are acceptable, accessible and useful. Existing examples of user involvement (see Chapter Three) should be more widely promoted.

■ A RANGE OF LEARNING OPPORTUNITIES

People with mental health difficulties are not an homogeneous group. Academic, vocational and non-vocational courses should be available to cater for these diverse needs and should be offered in a range of settings including colleges. adult education centres, hospitals, day centres and other community-based settings.

■ SUPPORT

Good support can be crucial in determining whether someone has a positive experience of education. A wide range of support strategies should be available, as part of the organisation's learning support service. Support should be responsive and non-stigmatising. It should offer choices to individuals and should focus on supporting people in the learning environment and maximising their learning opportunities.

■ PARTNERSHIPS

An inter-agency approach to the planning, resourcing, and delivery of education is essential in order to plan coherently (at an organisational and individual level) and to maximise available resources. Partnership working can have a positive impact on areas such as staff training and development, access, learner support and student recruitment.

■ FUNDING

No single service is likely to meet the needs of any one individual. A multi-agency approach is essential, with funding drawn from a variety of sources. A mixed funding package should be reviewed regularly, as the person's needs change.

■ LEADERSHIP

The commitment of senior managers is essential in creating effective strategies, based on an inclusive learning approach which can meet the needs and aspirations of all adult learners including people with mental health difficulties. Small-scale initiatives can be very successful but an organisation-wide strategy gives a clear signal that senior management is committed to inclusion.

■ STAFF DEVELOPMENT

Staff development is essential and training programmes should address the needs of all staff as part of the development of an inclusive approach. Staff in dedicated posts, tutors working in discrete provision and learning support staff should have regular access to training, supervision and other forms of support since this work can be stressful and staff need to take care of their own mental health.

■ QUALITY

Students with mental health difficulties are entitled to education provision which is of the same standard as that offered to all students. A range of quality checks should be used, including mechanisms which enable the organisation to ascertain students' views on their experiences of education.

■ LOOKING AHEAD

Educational opportunities for people with mental health difficulties are growing. This publication stems from a short-term project which we hope will lead to further developments. There is still a long way to go and NIACE, FEDA and SKILL hope to play a part in future developments.

APPENDIX A

REFERENCES/READING LIST

Alinsky, S. (1971) *Rules for Radicals.*

Ashurst, P. and Hall, Z. (1989) *Understanding Women in Distress.* Tavistock/Routledge.

Australian Government Publishing Service (1993) *Human Rights and Mental Illness: Report of the National Inquiry into Human Rights of People with Mental Illness.* AGPS.

Barker, I. and Peck, E. (eds) (1987) *Power in Strange Places: User Empowerment in Mental Health Services.* Good Practices in Mental Health.

Bates, P. (1995) 'What makes empowerment so difficult?', *Kent Journal of Practice Research,* Vol. 11. No. 1, October: 35-42. Social Services Research Strategy Group, Kent County Council.

Bates, P. (1996) 'Lessons for life', *Health Service Journal,* 3 October: 28.

Bee, E. and Martin, I. (1997) 'The educational dimensions of mental health work', *Adults Learning,* January: 128-31.

Beresford, P. and Croft, S. (1993) *Citizen Involvement: A Practical Guide for Change.* Macmillan.

Boulton, A. and Hatton, S. (1991) *On the Road to Participation: Educational Opportunities for People with Mental Health Problems or Mental Illness.* Somerset County Council/Workers' Educational Association (Western District).

Brailsford, D. (1993) 'Liverpool: a step further in adult education and mental health', *Educare,* June, 46: 14-16.

Centre for Economic Performance (1997) *Widening Participation in Further Education and Training: A Survey of the Issues.* Prepared for the FEFC's Learning Works Committee. CEP.

Corlett, S. and Dumbleton, P. (1992) 'The implications of the Further and Higher Education Act 1992 for students with disabilities and learning difficulties in England, Wales and Scotland', *Educare,* July, 43: 5-7

Deffley, W. (1996) 'Beyond the barriers', *Notes and Quotes,* January: 3. SKILL.

Department of Health (1989) *Caring for People. Community Care in the Next Decade and Beyond.* Cm. 849. HMSO.

Department of Health (1992) *The Health of the Nation: A Strategy for Health in England.* Cm. 1986. HMSO.

Department of Health (1992a) *Review of Health and Social Services for Mentally Disordered Offenders and Others Requiring Similar Services. Final Summary Report.* Cm. 2088. HMSO.

Department of Health (1996) *Mental Illness: Mental Health and Older People.* DoH: Health of the Nation.

Department of Health (1996a) *Mental Illness: Can Children and Young People have Mental Health Problems?* DoH: Health of the Nation.

Department of Health (1997) *Developing Partnerships in Mental Health.* Cm. 3555, HMSO.

Department of Health (1997a) *The Health of the Nation: Briefing Pack.* Second Edition. HMSO.

Depression Alliance (1997) *Student Stress Survival Pack.* Depression Alliance.

Disability on the Agenda (1995) *A Brief Guide to the Disability Discrimination Act.* DL40.

Disability on the Agenda (1996) *The Disability Discrimination Act: Definitions of Disability.* DL60

Disability on the Agenda (1996a) *The Disability Discrimination Act: Education.* DL100.

Fernando, S. (1995) *Mental Health in a Multi-Ethnic Society. A Multi-Disciplinary Handbook.* Routledge.

Foster, E.J. (1994) 'Some factors associated with the retention of students with mental health problems in community education', unpubl. M.Ed thesis.

Frado, L.M. (1993) *Learning Diversity: Accommodations in Colleges and Universities for Students with Mental Illness.* Canadian Association for Mental Health.

Further Education Funding Council (FEFC) (1996) *Inclusive Learning: Report of the Learning Difficulties and/or Disabilities Committee,* chaired by Professor John Tomlinson. FEFC.

Further Education Funding Council (FEFC) (1996a), *Inclusive Learning: Principles and Recommendations. A Summary of the Findings of the Learning Difficulties and/or Disabilities Committee.* FEFC.

Further Education Funding Council (FEFC) (1997) *Learning Works. Report of the Committee on Widening Participation.* FEFC.

Further Education Funding Council (FEFC) (1997a) 'Results of Consultation on the Implementation of Inclusive Learning', Circular 97/24. July. FEFC.

Further Education Funding Council (FEFC) (1997b) *Identifying and Addressing Needs. A Practical Guide.* FEFC.

Goldsmith, M. (1996) *Hearing the Voice of People with Dementia.* Jessica Kingsley Publishers.

Gosling, P. (1994) *A Little Bit of Freedom: A survey of what people with mental health problems want from education and training.* Southwark Day Care Forum.

Greatorex, H., Catherine, H., Beeforth, M. and Swirsky, H. (1993) 'The Education Programme: Adult Education as a Model for a Rehabilitation Day Service. Conference presentation, South Downs NHS Trust.

Green, G. (forthcoming) *Unemployed, with a Background of Mental Health Difficulties. What Chance Work?*

Hampshire County Council (with North Hampshire Mental Health Forum) (1994) 'Towards a better future: developing learning opportunities for people with mental health problems'. Conference report

Hewitson-Ratcliffe, C. (ed.) (1995) *Current Developments in Further Education. Report of Third John Baillie Memorial Conference.* SKILL.

Hooper, R. (1996) 'Adult education for mental health. A study in innovation and partnership', *Adults Learning*, 8, 3: pp. nos.

Hunter, D. (1997) 'Collective activity as a route to self-development', *Adults Learning*, April: 212-13.

Huxley, M. A. Vaughan (1993) 'Changes at home: Part II of the Walter Lessing Memorial Lecture, *Educare*, June, 46: 3-7.

Jenkins, A. (forthcoming) *Educational Guidance for Adults with Mental Health Difficulties.* University of Kent, Unit for Part-time Studies.

Jennings, S. (1996) *Creating Solutions. Developing Alternatives in Black Mental Health.* King's Fund.

Kennedy, H. (1997) 'Four cornerstones of Labour's new colossus', *Guardian*, 1 July, Schools supplement: 2-3.

Lancashire County Council (with Executive Business Channel) (1997) *Snakes and Ladders: Adult Education and Mental Health.* A Video-Based Action Pack based on the Lancashire Stepping Stones Programme.

Lanham, W., Spencer, C. and Williams, C. (1997) *College Link Programme: A Preliminary Evaluation.* Haringey Healthcare NHS Trust.

Leach, J. (1996) 'Integrating students with mental health problems into community education', unpublished paper.

Leach, J. (1996a) 'Developing people at RESTORE'. *Rehab Network*, Summer: 9-10.

Lindow, V. (1996) *Community Service Users as Consultants and Trainers (National User Involvement Project)*. NHS Executive, Community Care Branch.

Little, M. (1995) 'College success questionnaire. Development of an instrument for assessing students with mental health problems enrolling for college and to aid in the design of supported education programmes'. MSc dissertation (unpubl.)

Main, J. (1996) *Ballendon Education Project: An Education and Mental Health Initiative*. Stevenson College, Edinburgh.

Meager, N., Evans, C. and Dench, S. (1996) *Mapping Provision: The Provision of and Participation in Further Education by Students with Learning Difficulties and/or Disabilities*. A Report to the FEFC's Learning Difficulties and/or Disabilities Committee. HMSO

Mental Health Foundation (1997) *Knowing Our Own Minds: A survey of how people in emotional distress take control of their lives*. Mental Health Foundation.

NIACE (1994) *Learning Opportunities for Adults with Learning Difficulties and/or Disabilities. Evidence for the FEFC Committee of Enquiry*. NIACE.

NIACE (1995) *A Briefing on NIACE Research on Adult Participation and Barriers to Access. Presented to the FEFC Widening Participation Committee*. NIACE.

NIACE (1997) *Learning Works: A Briefing Sheet on the Learning Works (FEFC) Committee*. NIACE.

Open University (1994) *Supporting Students with Mental Health Difficulties. Guidelines for Tutorial and Counselling Staff*. Open University.

Open University (1996) *Training the Trainers Workshop No. 19. Mental Health: Helping not Hindering*. Open University.

Read, J. and Baker, S. (1996) *Not Just Sticks and Stones: A Survey of the Stigma, Taboos and Discrimination Experienced by People with Mental Health Problems*. MIND.

Ruddock, H. and Worrall, P. (1997) *Educational Project with MIND. Overcoming the Isolation of People with Mental Health Difficulties through Creative Writing and Literacy*. Dearne Valley College.

Scottish Further Education Unit (SFEU) (1994) *Mental Health Matters: Guidelines for Supporting Students with Mental Health Difficulties*. SFEU.

SKILL/Scottish Further Education Unit (1994) *Expanding the Boundaries: Readings in Mental Health and Education*. SKILL/SFEU.

SKILL (1997) *Disabled Students' Charter: A Challenge to the Political Parties*. SKILL.

Stuart, M. and Thomson, A. (1995) *Engaging with Difference. The 'Other' in Adult Education*. NIACE.

Tuckett, A. (1997) *Lifelong Learning in England and Wales. An Overview and Guide to Issues arising from the European Year of Lifelong Learning.* NIACE.

UNESCO (1994) *The Salamanca Statement and Framework for Action on Special Needs Education.* UNESCO.

Wertheimer, A. (1997) *Inclusive Education: A Framework for Change.* National and International Perspectives. Centre for Studies on Inclusive Education.

USEFUL ORGANISATIONS

African-Caribbean Mental Health Association
35-37 Electric Avenue
London SW9 8JP
0171 737 3603

Depression Alliance
PO Box 1022
London SE1 7QB
0171 721 7672

Further Education Development Agency (FEDA)
Citadel Place
Tinworth Street
London SE11 5EH
0171 962 1280

Further Education Funding Council (England)
Cheylesmore House
Quinton Road
Coventry CV1 2WT
01203 863000

Further Education Funding Council (Wales)
Lambourne House
Cardiff Business Park
Llanishen
Cardiff CF4 5GL
01222 761861

Good Practices in Mental Health
380-384 Harrow Road
London
W9 2HU
0171 289 2034

Mental Health Foundation
27 Mortimer Street
London WIN 8JU
0171 580 0145

Manic Depression Fellowship
8-10 High Street
Kingston upon Thames
KT1 1EY
0181 974 6550

MIND (National Association for Mental Health)
Granta House
15-19 The Broadway
London
E15 4BQ
0181 519 2122

National Schizophrenia Fellowship
28 Castle Street
Kingston upon Thames
Surrey
KT6 4NS
0181 547 3937

NIACE (The National Organisation for Adult Learning)
21 De Montfort Street
Leicester
LE1 7GE
0116 204 4200

SKILL (National Bureau for Students with Disabilities)
336 Brixton Road
London
SW9 7AA
0171 274 0565

Survivors Speak Out
34 Osnaburgh Street
London
NW1 3ND
0171 916 5472

UK Advocacy Network
Premier House
14 Cross Burgess Street
Sheffield
S1 2MG
0114 272 8171

Workers' Educational Association
Temple House
17 Victoria Park Square
London
E2 9PB
0181 983 1515

THE DISABILITY DISCRIMINATION ACT 1995: FURTHER EDUCATION

Definition of disability

The Act defines disability as:

> A physical or mental impairment which has a substantial and long-term adverse effect on a person's ability to carry out normal day-to-day activities.

Mental impairments include mental illness. People who have a disability, and people who have had a disability but no longer have one, are covered by the Act.

Education

This Act builds on the Further and Higher Education Acts of 1992 which require further education providers to take account of the needs of students with learning and other disabilities

The Disability Discrimination Act places a new duty on Further Education Funding Councils in England and Wales to:

> require further education colleges to publish disability statements and report to the Government on their future plans for providing further education to students with disabilities.

Disability statements will give information about facilities for disabled people. They can include:

> – the educational institution's policy towards disabled students

and the names of the people responsible for it;
– any special admission arrangements (to help students find out more about the application process and how their needs will be met);
– the institution's complaints procedures for disabled students.

Sources: Disability on the Agenda (1995, 1996, 1996a)

CASE STUDY VISITS

Abergavenny
- Gardd-y-Bryn

Adult College Peterborough

Ashworth (Special) Hospital

Barnet College

Blackpool & Fylde College

Bolton Community Education Service

Calderdale College (by telephone)

Cambridgeshire Local Education Authority

Cardiff
- Awetu
- Four Winds
- Meteor Street Day Services
- Ty Canna
- Whitchurch Hospital

City College Norwich

Clarendon College, Nottingham

East Riding Unity Authority

Lancashire STEPPING STONES (County Management)

Leicester REMIT Project

Leicester WEA

Lewisham Community Education Service

LIFT – Leicester College of Adult Education

Nelson & Colne College

Norfolk Local Education Authority

South Nottingham College, West Bridgford

Southwark College

Warrington Collegiate Institute

Warrington MIND

WEA York

West Nottinghamshire College, Mansfield

York College of Further & Higher Education

THE QUESTIONNAIRE

This Appendix shows copies of the questionnaires which were sent to local education authorities and further education colleges. The accompanying covering letter appears on the next page.

Respondents were also asked to complete a brief checklist giving their name and job title, as well as confirming details of their organisation's address and phone number. Additionally, FE colleges were asked to indicate the FEFC region to which they belonged.

All organisations to whom the questionnaire was sent received a note outlining the aims and focus of the joint NIACE/FEDA project. Colleges and authorities were asked to return their questionnaire even where there was no specific provision for adult with mental health difficulties.

 **Further Education
Development Agency**

Coombe Lodge
Blagdon
Bristol BS18 6RG

Telephone [01761] 462503
Facsimile [01761] 463104

2 July 1996

Dear Sir/Madam

Adult Learners and Mental Health (MO46)

FEDA is working in collaboration with NIACE to undertake a national project which aims to examine further and adult education provision for people with mental health difficulties. Research by both organisations has identified this as a particularly problematic area with many unmet needs yet little information is available on a national basis. The project will consist of a national survey of provision, case studies of effective practice, and will produce a guidance document for staff.

This letter is to ask for your assistance with this project, by asking you to complete the attached questionnaire. The research does not cover the full range of people with "learning difficulties" as defined in section 4 of the Further and Higher Education Act (1992). The focus is on adults who may be variously described, as indicated in the accompanying guidance notes.

The most appropriate person to complete this questionnaire is likely to be the staff member with designated responsibility for mental health, or the people who coordinate learning support in your establishment and they will need to liaise with the management information staff.

We appreciate how many requests for information you receive, including many questionnaires, but we would be most grateful for your response by **26 July 1996**. We know that colleges are dealing with difficult issues with little support, and there is little reliable information about educational provision for adults with mental health difficulties. This project aims to provide guidance and support in tackling a key area of participation, retention, and achievement.

Yours sincerely

Sally Faraday

Sally Faraday
(On behalf of the project team)

ADULT CONTINUING EDUCATION
AND PEOPLE WITH MENTAL HEALTH DIFFICULTIES

This form will be electronically scanned. It would be helpful if you would use black ink when completing it. Please mark appropriate tick boxes thus : ☑ *or write within the text boxes provided. If there is insufficient room for your written answers then please use the space at the end of the questionnaire, available for comments, or attach an additional sheet.*

POLICIES, STRATEGIC AND OPERATIONAL PLANNING

Q1 From 1996, the Disability Discrimination Act requires colleges to publish statements on their provision for students with disabilities. Does your statement make specific reference to students with mental health difficulties?

☐ Yes   ☐ No

Q2 (a) Does your strategic plan make specific reference to people with mental health difficulties?

☐ Yes *(Go to Q3)*   ☐ No

(b) If 'No', do you plan to do so?

☐ Yes   ☐ No

Q3 Do you have other written policy documents or guidance relating to students with mental health difficulties?

☐ Yes **(Please enclose a copy)**   ☐ No

Q4 (a) Were people with mental health difficulties involved in drawing up any of these documents?

☐ Yes   ☐ No *(Go to Q5)*

(b) If 'Yes', please describe how they were involved:

```



```

Q5 (a) Are you currently planning any new provision for people with mental health difficulties?

☐ Yes   ☐ No *(Go to Q6)*

Q5 (b) If 'Yes', please describe:

```



```

Further Education Development Agency

Q6 **How would you describe your college's approach to provision for students with mental health difficulties?**

	Strongly Disagree				Strongly Agree
This college is committed to making provision for adults with mental health difficulties on discrete courses.	☐	☐	☐	☐	☐
This college is committed to making provision for adults with mental health difficulties on mainstream courses.	☐	☐	☐	☐	☐
This college is committed to ensuring that students with mental health difficulties are appropriately supported.	☐	☐	☐	☐	☐

THE STUDENTS

Q7 **How does the college attempt to identify students with mental health difficulties?**

Other:

☐ Self-identification
☐ Referral sources (e.g. day centres)
☐ At the guidance interview
☐ At an additional support needs interview
☐ Tutors referring existing students
☐ Other (please also describe, opposite)

Q8 **What was the total number of FE students enrolled at the college at 30 June 1996? (Actual numbers, not FTE)**

Full-time [   ]   Part-time [   ]

Q9 **How many students enrolled at 30 June 1996 have been identified as having mental health difficulties?**

	Males	Females	Total
Full-time	[ ]	[ ]	[ ]
Part-time	[ ]	[ ]	[ ]

Q10 **How many students with mental health difficulties, enrolled at 30 June 1996, were in the following age groups?**

16-18	19-25	26-59	60+
[ ]	[ ]	[ ]	[ ]

Q11 How many students with mental health difficulties were enrolled at 30 June 1996?

	Full-time	Part-time
On discrete courses		
On mainstream courses (with support)		

Q12 (a) **Does the college make any provision specifically for adults with mental health difficulties from minority ethnic communities?**

☐ Yes   ☐ No   *(Go to Q13)*

(b)   **If 'Yes', please describe briefly how that provision is made:**

Q13 (a)   **Does the college specifically seek to recruit students with mental health difficulties?**

☐ Yes   ☐ No   *(Go to Q14)*

(b)   **If 'Yes', do you target any of the following groups:**   **Other groups targeted:**

☐ Young adults with mental health difficulties
☐ Day centre and day hospital users
☐ Adults resettled from long-stay hospitals
☐ Women with mental health difficulties
☐ Older people with mental health difficulties
☐ Other *(please also specify, opposite)*

Q14 Does the college use any of the following strategies to enable adults with mental health difficulties to access provision?   **Other strategies used:**

☐ Taster sessions and courses
☐ Targeted publicity (e.g. posters, leaflets)
☐ Making links with local mental health services
☐ College staff meeting mental health service users
☐ Contact with local mental health professionals
☐ Special assessment and enrolment arrangements
☐ Other *(please also specify, opposite)*

Q15 How do you identify the learning and support needs of students with mental health difficulties within the assessment process?

Q16 (a) Does the college operate any formal policies regarding grounds for exclusion (e.g. risk assessment, college-student contracts)?

☐ Yes   ☐ No   *(Go to Q17)*

(b) If 'Yes', please describe briefly:

CURRICULUM, ACCREDITATION AND PROGRESSION

Q17 How many students with mental health difficulties are enrolled on the following courses?

	less than 10	10-20	21-50	more than 50
GCSE / GCE	☐	☐	☐	☐
'A' level	☐	☐	☐	☐
NVQ	☐	☐	☐	☐
GNVQ	☐	☐	☐	☐
Other vocational courses	☐	☐	☐	☐
Basic skills (e.g. literacy, numeracy)	☐	☐	☐	☐
Personal skills	☐	☐	☐	☐
Other non-vocational courses	☐	☐	☐	☐

Q18 In the last two years, how many students with mental health difficulties have moved on to:

Full-time mainstream further / higher education

Part-time mainstream further / higher education

Paid employment

Unpaid employment

A more independent lifestyle

FUNDING

Q19 What funding did you receive in 1995/6 for provision for adults with mental health difficulties?

	less than £1,000	£1000- £5999	£6000- £20,000	over £20,000
FEFC (England and Wales)	☐	☐	☐	☐
Local Education Authority	☐	☐	☐	☐
Social Services Department	☐	☐	☐	☐
Mental Illness Specific Grant	☐	☐	☐	☐
Health authority / trust	☐	☐	☐	☐
Voluntary organisation	☐	☐	☐	☐
Charitable trust	☐	☐	☐	☐
European Community	☐	☐	☐	☐
Training and Enterprise Council	☐	☐	☐	☐
City Challenge	☐	☐	☐	☐
Joint Funding) *Please also*	☐	☐	☐	☐
Other) *specify, below*	☐	☐	☐	☐

Joint / Other funding details:

SUPPORT FOR STUDENTS

Q20 Which of the following types of support are currently available to students with mental health difficulties?

Other types of support:

- ☐ Learning support assistants
- ☐ Additional tutor support
- ☐ Additional tutorial time
- ☐ General student counselling service
- ☐ Guidance and counselling
- ☐ Transport between home and college
- ☐ NHS support (e.g. community psychiatric nurses)
- ☐ Social work support
- ☐ Drop-ins (off-course support)
- ☐ Peer support groups
- ☐ Buddy, volunteer or mentoring
- ☐ Other *(please also specify, opposite)*

Q21 Who currently provides this support?

Other provider:

- ☐ College teaching staff
- ☐ College's support staff / teaching assistants
- ☐ Other students / volunteers
- ☐ Local Education Authority
- ☐ Social Services Department
- ☐ Voluntary organisation
- ☐ Health authority / trust
- ☐ Other *(please also specify, opposite)*

Q22 Do you consider the overall support available to students with mental health difficulties at your college to be:

☐ Inadequate   ☐ Adequate   ☐ Well developed

Q23 (a)   Are there any particular support needs you feel are not being met at present?

☐ Yes   ☐ No   *(Go to Q24)*

(b)   If 'Yes', describe briefly what you see as the unmet needs:

```
```

Q24 Do you plan to address any of these unmet needs in the immediate future?

☐ Yes   ☐ No

STAFF SUPPORT AND TRAINING

Q25 How many staff in your college are working with adults with mental health difficulties?

Teaching staff [   ]   Support staff [   ]

Q26 Is there a designated member of staff responsible for students with mental health difficulties?

☐ Yes   ☐ No

Q27 (a)   Do college staff receive any training on working with students with mental health difficulties?

Teaching staff   Yes ☐   Support staff   Yes ☐
No ☐   No ☐

(b)   If 'Yes', please give brief details of the type of training (e.g. in house, external, accredited, etc.)

```
```

Further Education Development Agency

LIAISON WITH OTHER AGENCIES

Q28 (a) Do college staff have contact with the following agencies in relation to the needs of students with mental health difficulties?

Contact with other agencies:

	Yes	No
FE colleges	☐	☐
Local Education Authority	☐	☐
Social Services Department	☐	☐
Health authority / trust	☐	☐
GPs and primary care teams	☐	☐
Voluntary organisations	☐	☐
Mental health user groups	☐	☐
Training and Enterprise Council	☐	☐
Private mental health service providers	☐	☐
Other	☐	☐

(please also specify, opposite)

(b) If 'Yes', please give details of the form of contact (e.g. cross-college support network, regular meetings, telephone contact, shared training, handling referrals, etc.):

Q29 (a) Have college staff been involved in any inter-agency planning for people with mental health difficulties (e.g. local planning groups, joint care planning teams)?

Yes ☐   No ☐   *(Go to Q30)*

(b) If 'Yes', please list groups and include brief details of their activities:

Q30 Does your local authority Community Care Plan mention adult education in relation to people with mental health difficulties?

☐ Yes   ☐ No

Q31 During the next stage of the project we plan to visit about ten sites to document examples of good practice and explore the issues raised by this questionnaire survey in greater depth. Would you be willing to be considered as a study site?

☐ Yes   ☐ No

Q32 If there are any examples of interesting and/or innovative provision at your college for students with mental health difficulties, please would you describe them briefly below

Q33 If there are any further comments you wish to make about the provision of further education for adults with mental health difficulties, please use the space below.

THANK YOU FOR COMPLETING THE QUESTIONNAIRE

A FREEPOST envelope is enclosed for the return of the questionnaire, and any enclosures.
Please return by 26 July 1996 to:
Craig Dimmock, FEDA, FREEPOST, Coombe Lodge, Blagdon, Bristol BS18 6BR

ADULT CONTINUING EDUCATION
AND PEOPLE WITH MENTAL HEALTH DIFFICULTIES

This form will be electronically scanned. It would be helpful if you would use black ink when completing it. Please mark appropriate tick boxes thus : ☑ *or write within the text boxes provided. If there is insufficient room for your written answers then please use the space at the end of the questionnaire, available for comments, or attach an additional sheet.*

POLICIES, STRATEGIC AND OPERATIONAL PLANNING

Q1 From 1996, the Disability Discrimination Act requires LEAs to publish statements on their provision for students with disabilities. Does your statement make specific reference to students with mental health difficulties?

☐ Yes   ☐ No

Q2 **(a)** Has your LEA produced a strategic plan?

☐ Yes *[Go to (b)]*   ☐ No *[Go to (c)]*

(b) If 'Yes', does the plan make specific reference to people with mental health difficulties?

☐ Yes *[Go to Q3]*   ☐ No *[Go to Q3]*

(c) If 'No', do you intend producing a plan?

☐ Yes   ☐ No

Q3 Does the LEA have other written policy documents or guidance relating to students with mental health difficulties?

☐ Yes *(Please enclose a copy)*   ☐ No

Q4 **(a)** Were people with mental health difficulties involved in drawing up any of these documents?

☐ Yes   ☐ No *(Go to Q5)*

(b) If 'Yes', please describe how they were involved:

```

```

Q5 **(a)** Are you currently planning any new provision for people with mental health difficulties?

☐ Yes   ☐ No *(Go to Q6)*

Q5 **(b)** If 'Yes', please describe:

```

```

Further Education Development Agency

Q6 How would you describe your LEA's approach to provision for students with mental health difficulties?

	Strongly Disagree				Strongly Agree
This LEA is committed to making provision for adults with mental health difficulties on discrete courses.	☐	☐	☐	☐	☐
This LEA is committed to making provision for adults with mental health difficulties on mainstream courses.	☐	☐	☐	☐	☐
This LEA is committed to ensuring that students with mental health difficulties are appropriately supported.	☐	☐	☐	☐	☐

THE STUDENTS

Q7 How does the LEA attempt to identify students with mental health difficulties?

Other:

☐ Self-identification
☐ Referral sources (e.g. day centres)
☐ At the guidance interview
☐ At an additional support needs interview
☐ Tutors referring existing students
☐ Other *(please also describe, opposite)*

Q8 What was the total number of FE students in adult education provision enrolled with the LEA at 30 June 1996? (Actual numbers, not FTE)

Full-time ☐   Part-time ☐

Q9 How many students enrolled on LEA courses at 30 June 1996 have been identified as having mental health difficulties?

	Males	Females	Total
Full-time			
Part-time			

Q10 How many students with mental health difficulties, enrolled at 30 June 1996, were in the following age groups?

16-18	19-25	26-59	60+

Q11 How many students with mental health difficulties were enrolled at 30 June 1996?

	Full-time	Part-time
On discrete courses		
On mainstream courses (with support)		

Q12 (a)   Does the LEA make any provision specifically for adults with mental health difficulties from minorities ethnic communities?

☐ Yes   ☐ No   *(Go to Q13)*

(b)   If 'Yes', please describe briefly how that provision is made:

Q13 (a)   Does the LEA specifically seek to recruit students with mental health difficulties?

☐ Yes   ☐ No   *(Go to Q14)*

(b)   If 'Yes', do you target any of the following groups:

Other groups targeted:

☐ Young adults with mental health difficulties
☐ Day centre and day hospital users
☐ Adults resettled from long-stay hospitals
☐ Women with mental health difficulties
☐ Older people with mental health difficulties
☐ Other *(please also specify, opposite)*

Q14 Does the LEA use any of the following strategies to enable adults with mental health difficulties to access provision?

Other strategies used:

☐ Taster sessions and courses
☐ Targeted publicity (e.g. posters, leaflets)
☐ Making links with local mental health services
☐ LEA staff meeting mental health service users
☐ Contact with local mental health professionals
☐ Special assessment and enrolment arrangements
☐ Other *(please also specify, opposite)*

Q15 How do you identify the learning and support needs of students with mental health difficulties within the assessment process?

Q16 (a) Does the LEA operate any formal policies regarding grounds for exclusion (e.g. risk assessment, college-student contracts)?

☐ Yes   ☐ No   *(Go to Q17)*

(b) If 'Yes', please describe briefly:

CURRICULUM, ACCREDITATION AND PROGRESSION

Q17 How many students with mental health difficulties are enrolled on the following courses?

	less than 10	10-20	21-50	more than 50
GCSE / GCE	☐	☐	☐	☐
'A' level	☐	☐	☐	☐
NVQ	☐	☐	☐	☐
GNVQ	☐	☐	☐	☐
Other vocational courses	☐	☐	☐	☐
Basic skills (e.g. literacy, numeracy)	☐	☐	☐	☐
Personal skills	☐	☐	☐	☐
Other non-vocational courses	☐	☐	☐	☐

Q18 In the last two years, how many students with mental health difficulties have moved on to:

Full-time mainstream further / higher education

Part-time mainstream further / higher education

Paid employment

Unpaid employment

A more independent lifestyle

FUNDING

Q19 **What funding did you receive in 1995/6 for provision for adults with mental health difficulties?**

	less than £1,000	£1000- £5999	£6000- £20,000	over £20,000
FEFC (England and Wales)				
Local Education Authority				
Social Services Department				
Mental Illness Specific Grant				
Health authority / trust				
Voluntary organisation				
Charitable trust				
European Community				
Training and Enterprise Council				
City Challenge				
Joint Funding) *Please also*				
Other) *specify, below*				

Joint / Other funding details:

SUPPORT FOR STUDENTS

Q20 **Which of the following types of support are currently available to students with mental health difficulties?**

Other types of support:

- Learning support assistants
- Additional tutor support
- Additional tutorial time
- General student counselling service
- Guidance and counselling
- Transport between home and college
- NHS support (e.g. community psychiatric nurses)
- Social work support
- Drop-ins (off-course support)
- Peer support groups
- Buddy, volunteer or mentoring
- Other *(please also specify, opposite)*

Q21 **Who currently provides this support?**

Other provider:

- LEA teaching staff
- LEA support staff / teaching assistants
- Other students / volunteers
- Local Education Authority
- Social Services Department
- Voluntary organisation
- Health authority / trust
- Other *(please also specify, opposite)*

Q22 Do you consider the overall support available to students with mental health difficulties at your LEA to be:

☐ Inadequate   ☐ Adequate   ☐ Well developed

Q23 (a)   Are there any particular support needs you feel are not being met at present?

☐ Yes   ☐ No   *(Go to Q24)*

(b)   If 'Yes', describe briefly what you see as the unmet needs:

```
[blank box]
```

Q24 Do you plan to address any of these unmet needs in the immediate future?

☐ Yes   ☐ No

STAFF SUPPORT AND TRAINING

Q25 How many staff in your LEA are working with adults with mental health difficulties?

Teaching staff [   ]   Support staff [   ]

Q26 Is there a designated member of staff responsible for students with mental health difficulties?

☐ Yes   ☐ No

Q27 (a)   Do LEA employees receive any training on working with students with mental health difficulties?

Teaching staff   Yes ☐   Support staff   Yes ☐
                  No   No

(b)   If 'Yes', please give brief details of the type of training (e.g. in house, external, accredited, etc.)

```
[blank box]
```

LIAISON WITH OTHER AGENCIES

Q28 (a)   Do LEA staff have contact with the following agencies in relation to the needs of students with mental health difficulties?

Contact with other agencies:

	Yes	No
FE colleges	☐	☐
Social Services Department	☐	☐
Health authority / trust	☐	☐
GPs and primary care teams	☐	☐
Voluntary organisations	☐	☐
Mental health user groups	☐	☐
Training and Enterprise Council	☐	☐
Private mental health service providers	☐	☐
Other		

(please also specify, opposite)

(b)   If 'Yes', please give details of the form of contact (e.g. cross-college support network, regular meetings, telephone contact, shared training, handling referrals, etc.):

Q29 (a)   Have LEA staff been involved in any inter-agency planning for people with mental health difficulties (e.g. local planning groups, joint care planning teams)?

☐ Yes   ☐ No   *(Go to Q30)*

(b)   If 'Yes', please list groups and include brief details of their activities:

Q30 Does your local authority Community Care Plan mention adult education in relation to people with mental health difficulties?

☐ Yes   ☐ No

Were LEA staff involved in drawing up the local authority's Community Care Plan?

☐ Yes   ☐ No

Q31 During the next stage of the project we plan to visit about ten sites to document examples of good practice and explore the issues raised by this questionnaire survey in greater depth. Would you be willing to be considered as a study site?

☐ Yes ☐ No

Q32 If there are any examples of interesting and/or innovative provision in your LEA for students with mental health difficulties, please would you describe them briefly below

Q33 If there are any further comments you wish to make about the provision of further education for adults with mental health difficulties, please use the space below.

THANK YOU FOR COMPLETING THE QUESTIONNAIRE

A FREEPOST envelope is enclosed for the return of the questionnaire, and any enclosures. Please return by 26 July 1996 to :
Craig Dimmock, FEDA, FREEPOST, Coombe Lodge, Blagdon, Bristol BS18 6BR

Further Education Development Agency

Also available from NIACE:

Adults with learning difficulties – Education for choice and empowerment
Jeannie Sutcliffe

NIACE/Open University Press ISBN 0 335 09609 3 £13.99

A book highlighting good practice in continuing education for adults with learning difficulties. Themes explored include self-advocacy and citizen advocacy; learning choices; ways and means of learning; reasons for learning; transition to community living; and educating the wider community.

Enabling learning – A student-centred approach to teaching adults with learning difficulties
Jeannie Sutcliffe

NIACE   ISBN 1 872941 91 5   £100.00

A staff development pack of thirteen modules including values and attitudes; inter-agency working; equal opportunities; assessment; planning and recording learning; progression and accreditation; and learning materials. Materials may be photocopied for use in training programmes.

Towards inclusion – developing integrated education for adults with learning difficulties
Jeannie Sutcliffe

NIACE   ISBN 1 872941 90 7   £100.00

A staff development pack of twelve modules including policy and practice; funding, mapping and networking; publicity; supporting students and tutors; evaluation; and action planning. For people who want to develop inclusive learning for adults with learning difficulties in further education colleges, adult education centres, social service day centres, health trusts and voluntary organisations.

SPECIAL OFFER

10% off when you order *Enabling learning* and *Towards inclusion* together. Normally available at £200, this offer gives you the opportunity to pay only £180 for these excellent staff development packs.

Adults learning

The need for a professional journal for all those concerned with adult learning has never been greater than before. The majority of students in further and higher education in Britain are adults. More and more awareness of adults as learners is being shown by government, the media, employers and trade unions. In a quickly-changing environment it is vital to keep abreast of current issues and initiatives, debates and events.

Adults learning is the only-UK-wide monthly journal devoted solely to issues of adult learning. It carries the latest news on policy and practice, and is published ten times a year by NIACE. It is a forum for the exchange of information and for networking and sharing good practice: essential reading for anyone who is serious about adult education and training.

UK Subscription rates: £40.00 (organisations); extra copies @ £15.00 each
                          £25.00 (individuals)
                          £15.00 (concessions for part-time tutors and adult learners)

ISSN 0955 2308

A free NIACE publications catalogue is available on request:
NIACE, 21 De Montfort Street, Leicester, LE1 7GE
Alternatively, visit the NIACE website on the Internet at
http://www.niace.org.uk